IN HONOR OF THE
CHARLESTON 9

IN HONOR OF THE CHARLESTON 9

A STUDY OF CHANGE FOLLOWING TRAGEDY

DR. DAVID GRIFFIN

First Edition

Griffin, David
In Honor of the Charleston 9: A Study of Change Following Tragedy.

ISBN-13: 978-1493735549   ISBN-10: 1493735543
BISAC: Education / Research

Ordering Information
www.drdavidgriffin.com

10 9 8 7 6 5 4 3 2 1

It's go time . . .

DEDICATION

This study is dedicated to Captain Mike Benke, Captain Billy Hutchinson, Captain Louis Mulkey, Engineer Mark Kelsey, Engineer Brad Baity, Assistant Engineer Michael French, Firefighter Earl Drayton, Firefighter Brandon Thompson, and Firefighter Melvin Champaign. These nine brave firefighters lost their lives on June 18, 2007 in Charleston, South Carolina as they battled a furniture warehouse fire. I will never forget what I have learned from you since that tragic day in 2007. I will give everything I have to fulfill the promise I made to all of you. I hope that when I get to see all of you again one day that I can look you in the eye and you are proud of what we have done together. Your lives will always be honored, and I will give my last breath to ensure your lives were not lost in vain. Rest in peace, brothers. You are in my heart and on my mind every day.

This study is also dedicated to the great men and women of The City of Charleston (SC) Fire Department. What you have been able to accomplish since 2007 is truly astounding. Your resilience, passion, dedication, and determination indicate your commitment to not only honoring the fallen, but your commitment to change as well. I am truly thankful to serve with each and every one of you in our great organization. God bless you and all of your families.

ACKNOWLEDGMENTS

To the love of my life, Melissa: You are an incredible woman and I do not know what I would do without your love and support. Through all of the pain, anger, tears, sleepless nights, and worry, you did not leave my side. You kept me strong on days I wanted to give up. I love you with every ounce of my being and I am so blessed that we will grow old together. I love you more as every day passes.

Mom and Dad: Thank you for always being there for me. Your love, support, and guidance have made me the man I am today. I love you very much.

Chief Thomas Carr: You allowed us to make change possible with your incredible vision. We will never be able to thank you enough. Rest in Peace.

Dr. Trish Dolasinski: Your guidance and passion during this process was incredible. There were days when I did not know where to go next. Without your expertise, I would still be sitting at my desk in tears trying to wrap my head around the dynamics involved in a study of this magnitude. Thank you so much, Dr. Trish.

TABLE OF CONTENTS

List of Tables   x
List of Figures   xii
Author's Note   xiii
Chapter 1   1
    Introduction   1
    Background of the Study   3
    Problem Statement   12
    Purpose of the Study   17
    Research Question(s)   21
    Advancing Scientific Knowledge   24
    Significance of the Study   28
    Rationale for Methodology   31
    Nature of the Research Design for the Study   35
    Definition of Terms   39
    Assumptions, Limitations, Delimitations   41
    Summary and Organization of the Remainder of the Study   44
Chapter 2   46
    Introduction to the Chapter and Background to the Problem   46
    Theoretical Foundations   53
    Review of the Literature   58
    Organizational Crisis   59
    Leadership and Planning   63
    Organizational Learning   79

Employee Learning and Development   81

Summary   88

Chapter 3   91

Introduction   91

Statement of the Problem   92

Research Question(s)   92

Research Methodology   95

Research Design   98

Population and Sample Selection   103

Sources of Data   107

Validity   110

Reliability   115

Data Collection Procedures   118

Data Analysis Procedures   121

Ethical Considerations   123

Limitations   124

Summary   125

Chapter 4   127

Introduction   127

Descriptive Data   128

Results   142

Research Question 1 (R1)   143

DLOQ Responses   143

Interviews   146

Artifact Data   150

Research Question 2 (R2)   155

DLOQ Responses   155

Interviews   159

Artifact Data   160

Research Question 3 (R3)   163

DLOQ Responses   163

Interviews   172

Artifact Data   176

Themes   189

Outline of Relationships of the Themes   190

Summary   192

Chapter 5   **199**

Introduction   199

Summary of the Study   201

Summary of Findings and Conclusion   204

Summary of Findings   204

Conclusion   210

Implications   213

Theoretical Implications   217

Practical Implications   218

Future Implications   219

Recommendations   220

Recommendations for Future Research   221

Recommendations for Practice   222

Epilogue   **224**

References   **I**

Appendix A   **XXIII**

Appendix B   **XXIV**

Appendix C   **XXV**

Appendix D   **XXVI**

Appendix E   **XXXI**

Appendix F   **XXXII**

LIST OF TABLES

Table 1

Fit Indices for Alternative Measurement Models in the Simple and Complex Factor Structures of Learning Construct for Exploratory and Confirmatory Samples   113

Table 2

Fit Indices for Alternative Measurement Models in the Simple and Complex Factor Structures of Performance Outcome for Exploratory and Confirmatory Samples   114

Table 3

Means, Standard Deviations, Reliabilities and Zero-Order Intercorrelations Among Dimensions of the Learning Organization   116

Table 4

Reliability Estimates for the Measures in the DLOQ   117

Table 5

Case Study Participants   130

Table 6

Legend   135

Table 7

Domain-Code Names and Descriptions   138

Table 8

Codes by Question from the DLOQ and Interviews   141

Table 9

DLOQ Individual Level Questions and Participant Mean

Ratings   145

Table 10

DLOQ Team Level Questions and Participant Mean

Ratings   158

Table 11

DLOQ Organizational Level Questions and Participant

Mean Ratings   167

Table 12

DLOQ Organizational Level Questions and Participant

Mean Ratings   171

LIST OF FIGURES

Figure 1. Conceptual Model   **192**

AUTHOR'S NOTE

When I was growing up, I never imagined that I would be a firefighter. Today, I can't imagine not being one. It was not in my blood, but it was always in my heart.

In 2004, after my interview with The City of Charleston (SC) Fire Department (CFD), I walked through the oldest working fire station in the United States. As I passed through the historical brick archways into the stall that housed the fire engines, I smelled the remnants of fire in the air. The floor still had the grooves from where the horses used to pull the steamer; hence the reason why it is called a stall, not a bay. I looked around and saw all of the firefighters gear hanging on the outside of the rig as if something was going to catch fire at any moment. The background noise echoed of words from the dispatcher that I could not yet understand. Tongue and groove woodwork lined the walls and ceiling of this landmark station that was placed in service in 1888.

"Wow, this is crazy. Think of all of the firefighters who have passed under these arches and served this remarkable city for over a hundred years," I said to myself, cheesing ear to ear.

I was in awe. I had the opportunity to be a part of something bigger than me and join a long line of firefighters who protected the city where I was born and raised. A mere 1.4 miles away, in the shadows of this station, I came into the world in the fall of 1980. Like I said, it was not in my blood, but it was always in my heart . . .from the first breath I took at Roper Hospital in downtown Charleston.

Little did I know that 27 years later I would respond to the most significant emergency in the history of the department. The date was June 18, 2007, and I was the acting engineer on the first due engine. Nine firefighters perished that day, and many lives were changed forever.

Personally, I saw things that I will never be able to forget. I blamed myself and turned to a life of alcohol, painkillers, and mixed martial arts fighting to cope. I shut out my family and friends as I searched for answers following this tragedy. Change was becoming an everyday occurrence in the CFD, and at first, I resisted it with every ounce of my being. I turned a blind eye to new tactics and training as I thought they would make me soft. As I look back, I am very ashamed of that time in my life.

Following a mixed martial arts contest against Ultimate Fighting Championship (UFC) fighter Houston "The Assassin" Alexander, I sat in darkness for three days with my eyes swollen shut. I realized that I was not honoring the fallen firefighters or helping the men and women of the CFD. I made a decision at the end of these life-changing 72 hours that I would stop feeling sorry for myself and make a difference. Once I could see again, my mission began. I enrolled in a doctoral program one month later determined to find answers to my questions. I knew scientific research was the only way.

Over the next three years, this research study was completed with the assistance of numerous advisors, professors, editors, and consultants from around the country who specialize in both the academic and emergency services fields. Professors from Harvard and Yale were then utilized to verify the qualitative methodology and edit the manuscript. Following this, an Academic Quality Review was performed by professors from Grand Canyon University (GCU) in Phoenix, Arizona. Finally, the Institutional Review Board at GCU approved the study for publication. From this work, I earned a Doctorate of Education in organizational leadership and development.

As you read this book, I ask you to keep an open mind and remember, this is **not a story.** This is a scientific research study indicating how an emergency services organization and its members recovered and changed following a multiple line of duty death (LODD) incident. Over the next five chapters, you will read repeated information as scientific research requires the reiteration of current literature on the studied topic, how the study was conducted, the results of the study, and how the results are beneficial. Specifically, this study will help other organizations combat organizational crisis or prevent it altogether with organizational learning. Again, this is a textbook of research, **not a story.**

This book represents my research and does not represent the views of the City of Charleston. Being immersed in this research for many years and actively being a part of the change process in the CFD, I believe *In Honor of The Charleston 9* to be an accurate portrayal of the events described. This is solely my work.

In closing, the changes that have taken place in the CFD are truly monumental. Do we still have work to complete for continued advancement? Of course we do. No organization is perfect. However, the men and women of the CFD should be proud of the progress that has been made. It is due to their hard work and dedication that we continue to improve on a daily basis. I am so proud and honored to serve with the brave men and women of the CFD. I would lay my life down for every one of them.

This study is in honor of the fallen, their families, and all of my fellow City of Charleston firefighters. We can and will be great. This proves what we are capable of.

—Griff

CHAPTER 1
Introduction to the Study

INTRODUCTION

The City of Charleston Fire Department (CFD) experienced an organizational crisis after the June 18, 2007 multiple line of duty death (LODD) incident in which nine firefighters perished in a furniture warehouse fire. Subsequent investigations performed by The Occupational Safety and Health Administration (OSHA), *The Routley Report* consultants (2008), and The National Institute of Standards and Technology (NIST) indicated the causal factors that took many lives included outdated equipment and firefighting techniques. Due to these investigations and the media attention that followed, the department faced an organizational crisis. The operations and leadership of the department were in need of complete revamping in order to meet the rigor and requirements of national best practices. Additionally, a nationally recognized fire chief was hired to navigate the CFD during these times of grave need.

The continuing failure of organizations to learn from times of organizational crisis creates political, social, financial, and individual costs that are attributable to the misunderstanding of learning processes (Elliot, 2009). The identification of failure and ways to avoid their repetition are most notably found with public inquiries (Gephardt, 2007). These types of public inquiries have proven to be major parts of the history of numerous organizational crises in an attempt to combat technological problems (Gephardt, 2007). The CFD experienced these aforementioned major costs and was forced to undergo numerous public inquiries before the firefighters and citizens, as well as the remaining stakeholders, felt confident with the direction and job performance of the organization.

While this organizational crisis led to years of negative feelings towards the CFD, the results prove to be worth the crisis, with the CFD now being a national model for other fire service organizations to follow. Many changes ensued following the tragedy caused by this crisis. Maitlis and Sonenshein (2010) indicated that there has been little integration between organizational crisis and organizational change. This is an area that was unknown and needed to be expanded upon to ensure the growth of the body of knowledge of organizational crisis and organizational learning.

It was not known how an organization like the CFD learned from an organizational crisis at the individual, team, and organizational levels. There is a gap in the literature relative to organizational crisis and organizational learning following this type of crisis. Specifically, this study investigated how the CFD learned from the organizational crisis of the June 18, 2007 incident through organizational learning. It is the expectation that future firefighters' lives will be saved from the investigations and results obtained from this study. Permission was granted to the researcher to perform this study via a site authorization form (Appendix A, on page XXIII).

The remainder of Chapter 1 includes multiple sections that are important to the study. These sections begin with the background of the study, which offers the reader the opportunity to become familiar with previous research regarding organizational crisis and organizational learning. Further, sections devoted to the problem statement and the purpose of the study are included to indicate the reason(s) that there is a need for this study. The rationale for methodology is also described to introduce the reader to the study's methodology, and why this methodology was an appropriate approach for this research.

Once the methodology is introduced, advancing scientific knowledge identifies the gap in previous research to indicate how this study increases the body of knowledge of organizational crisis and organizational learning. The research questions and the significance of the study follow the aforementioned and indicate specifically what the researcher is attempting to ascertain from the study. A section devoted to the definitions of important terms is provided to offer the reader an explanation of terms that are incorporated throughout the study. Finally, sections devoted to the assumptions, limitations, and delimitations, as well as a summary and organization for the remainder of the study are included.

BACKGROUND OF THE STUDY

Snyder, Hall, Robertson, Jasinski, and Miller (2006) stated that an organizational crisis is a condition that is considered extraordinary, damaging, and disruptive to an organization's state of operations. Although they are high impact events that have a low probability of occurring, they impose threats on the accountability and reliability of an organization (Tieyang, Sengul, & Lester, 2008). Furthermore, an organizational crisis is characterized by "ambiguity of cause, effect, and means of resolution" (Tieyang et al., 2008, p. 452). Research indicated that under specific conditions, negative impacts stemming from an organizational crisis in one organization could spread to another organization in the same industry (Tieyang et al., 2008). Additionally, the public nature of an organizational crisis and organizations' need to survive organizational crisis have gained increasing scholarly attention (Dutton & Jackson, 1987; Shrivastava, Mitroff, Miller, & Miglani, 1988). Regardless of this intensive attention, the effect of such a crisis upon those institutions in the same field is scant (Tieyang et al., 2008).

Many organizations have faced or will face crises that lead to grave consequences. Lin, Xia, Ismail, and Carley (2006) stated that organizational crises are becoming more inevitable due to the increase of complexity and technology-based processes in organizations. Furthermore, organizations are presented accident-triggered and technology-based crises that result in disasters if not properly handled (Lin et al., 2006). Perrow (1984) and Rochlin (1991) indicated that crises are bound to take place more specifically in large, complex systems. These crises predominantly stem from the external environment and organizational malfunctions (Perrow, 1984).

Previous studies have found evidence that can help organizations recover and grow from the grave consequences of an organizational crisis with learning. James' (2007) study on NASA's crisis indicated that the organization learned from their previous lack of transparency following the Challenger disaster. This gave them the knowledge to combat a future organizational crisis following the Columbia disaster.

According to Larson, Bengtsson, Henriksson, and Sparks (1998), increased levels of inter-organizational learning are possible with cultures that are more open. For example, James (2007) indicated that NASA's response following the Columbia tragedy was much more effective than their response following the Challenger incident. A few hours after the Columbia tragedy, NASA's leadership stated that they did not know what happened, which reflects the learning of a substantial lesson following the Challenger explosion when NASA's leadership created a suspicious and closed organizational climate (James, 2007). This overt willingness of the organizations leaders to shift to a more communication friendly environment assisted in crisis management following the disaster, resulting in reflection on the part of NASA's leadership that opened to a greater understanding of the value of transparency as they evaluated previous errors (James, 2007). Additionally, this increased media and public support for the organization, and allowed organizational members to express their opinions throughout the crisis stages following the Columbia disaster (James, 2007).

Another example of organizational crisis dates back to September 1982, when Johnson and Johnson, the makers of Tylenol, experienced a devastating event with one of their products (Simola, 2005). Boatright (2000) indicated that this event turned into an organizational crisis because of the seven deaths that were associated with the ingestion of Extra Strength Tylenol contaminated with cyanide. This crisis caused public outrage that could have been life-threatening to the Tylenol brand if executives did not act quickly (Simola, 2005). Collins and Porras (2000) stated that Johnson and Johnson issued an immediate nationwide product recall, even though the contamination seemed to be in one small geographical area. This product recall cost Johnson and Johnson over $100 million dollars and proved to the public that they were committed to the safety of their customers. This resulted in a strengthening of the public trust, as well as having a positive impact on market shares and sales (Fink 1986; Siomkos, 1992). Johnson and Johnson executives were compelled to develop an understanding of the problem and encourage the organization to learn and make the appropriate changes.

Critical information was not known, resulting in failure on the part of some organizations in managing their own crises effectively. An example of this was the Haitian government's response to the Earthquake that struck Haiti in 2010. As stated by Piotrowski (2010), the Earthquake in Haiti created a crisis of critical and immediate needs for the afflicted population. However, due to turf wars and interagency conflict, the appropriate actions were not taken by the organizations tasked with filling these needs (Piotrowski, 2010).

Another example predating the aforementioned event was the response to Hurricane Katrina in 2005. Farazmand (2007) revealed such a response to be a major failure that created a large-scale mismanagement and leadership crisis. These crises could have been managed more effectively if a coordinated planning structure and effective organizational management atmosphere were created where command had certain responsibilities based on priority and an appropriate timeframe (Dynes, 1970; Piotrowski, 2010). These plans may assist in managing crises effectively, however, as the Katrina and Haitian Earthquake events prove, if the plans are not in place and ready for implementation well preceding the crisis, an organization will not be able to learn and manage their own crisis effectively (Piotrowski, 2010).

According to the research that reflects the increased quality of decision-making outcomes from the previous actions of organizations, the concept of organizational learning is ever-expanding (Lynn, Simpson, & Souder, 1997). Furthermore, research suggested that more advanced methods of organizing facts regarding previous products or services are associated with better designs (Lynn et al., 1997). Considering this research for a public service organization such as the one studied, the new product developed is the increased quality of service provided by the more qualified and better-trained responders.

The aforementioned theory can be applied to the problems that the CFD faced. First, when the tragic event occurred, citizens were made aware of the outdated and unsafe practices and equipment utilized by the CFD. Once these reports began to spread via media outlets, as well as independent studies on the event, concerns were raised regarding the service that the CFD provided. This is similar to Simola's (2005) research on the Tylenol crisis in 1982. For decades the public trusted Tylenol to produce a quality product. However, after the contaminated items were recognized, Johnson and Johnson had to take drastic measures to instill trust again. The CFD had to do this as well post June 18, 2007. The first major step in doing so was to hire a new leader that would guide the organization during this time of reconstruction.

Lopez, Montes Peon, and Ordas (2006) stated that some organizational failures could be attributed to lacking management of organizational learning, which relates to the unsatisfactory management of organizational knowledge. Garvin, Edmondson, and Gino (2008) suggested that one of the most important aspects of a dynamic and evolutionary organization is that the organization must be a true learning organization. This type of organization facilitates the learning of its members, transforms itself continuously, and presents favorable organizational learning conditions (Lahteenmaki, Toivonen, & Mattila, 2001; Pedler, Bourgoyne, & Boydell, 1991).

Senge (1990) found specific evidence of how an organization can become a learning organization, and through the learning of individual members, organizations can change. Furthermore, organizational transformation can be created from members that develop organizational forms that focus on a learning environment (Dodgson, 1993). Therefore, if an organization can increase their organizational learning ability, favorable individual learning will be created as well (Cummings & Worley, 1997; Lahteenmaki et al., 2001). Moreover, an advanced degree of organizational learning, including the adoption of new mental models and matching behaviors, is needed to create a learning organization (Lahteenmaki et al., 2001; Senge, 1990).

These constructs are relevant to this study. For example, the CFD is a fire service organization that responds to emergency events such as EMS, fire, HAZMAT, and rescue. Similar to the research of Tieyang et al. (2008) on organizational crisis, the CFD's emergency events are high impact events that have a low probability of occurring. However, they impose threats on the accountability and reliability of the organization. Due to these types of events, if the organization does not respond successfully, an organizational crisis may ensue. Research indicated that an organizational crisis is considered extraordinary, damaging, and disruptive to the state of operations of an organization (Tieyang et al., 2008). Therefore, researching how the CFD responded to an organizational crisis is consistent with adding to the body of knowledge of this construct.

Organizational learning directly relates to the current study as well. Lynn et al. (1997) posited that organizational learning enables organizations to make better future decisions based on previous actions (Lynn et al., 1997). Further research suggested that more advanced methods of organizing facts regarding previous products or services are associated with better designs (Lynn et al., 1997). As a result of the investigation regarding how the CFD learned from such an organizational crisis at the individual, team, and organizational levels, evidence is gathered relative to the possibility of improved quality decision-making as an outcome of the increase of product by the CFD.

According to Scanlan (2011), organizational learning is accomplished by the direct focus of an entire organization toward changing a system rather than providing attention toward change at the individual level. Aslam, Javaid, Tanveer, Khan, and Shabbir (2011) indicated that organizational learning focuses on the mutual agreement of exploring new ideas, creating knowledge that can be shared, and finding solutions. Martin and Brun (2009) added that organizational learning occurs for different reasons. If there is a need, these reasons include system change development and team building (Argyris, 1990; Aslam et al., 2011; Denton, 1998; Senge, 1990).

Further, according to Denton (1998), system change development is needed when learning must take place to initiate organizational development that brings change to an organization's patterns and behaviors, ensuring improved competitive intelligence and organizational performance. In addition, Argyris (1990) indicated that organizational learning is needed when an organization wishes to incorporate new ethics, strategies, rules, regulations, and policies into an organization. Finally, Senge (1990) argued that an important addition for organizational learning is team building because when team building is practiced, employees begin to think as a system rather than as an individual. This allows for a collaborative culture and develops team learning as well.

Goh (1998) identified five strategic building blocks at the core of a learning organization. These include support and clarity for organizational vision, the mission to follow the vision, shared leadership, a culture devoted to experimentation, the open transfer of knowledge throughout an organization, cooperation, and teamwork. Two important foundations support these building blocks. The first foundation includes a design that is effective for the organization and aligns with the aforementioned building blocks. The other foundation consists of employees that obtain the appropriate competencies and skills required to perform the roles and tasks incorporated in the building blocks (Yang, Watkins, & Marsick, 2004).

Previous studies have utilized an instrument entitled Dimensions of the Learning Organization Questionnaire (DLOQ) created by Watkins and Marsick (1993, 1996, 1997), and reprinted in Marsick and Watkins (2003), to measure a learning organization. Research indicates that this instrument includes an inclusive and clear definition of the constructs of a learning organization and is defined from the perspective of organizational culture, including sufficient measurement regarding scale construction (Yang et al., 2004). More importantly, it incorporated a learning organization's dimensions at all levels including the individual, team, and organizational levels.

While reviewing many measurement tools that focus on the learning organization, Redding (1997) indicated that Watkins and Marsick's (1997) instrument was one of few that included all levels of learning: individual, team, and organizational. Another advantage for the use of this instrument in learning organization studies is that it integrates the main dimensions of a learning organization in a theoretical framework, as well as the identification of them in the literature (Yang et al., 2004). This type of theoretical framework offers important guidelines for the development and validation of instruments, as well as suggestions for further organizational studies.

There are gaps presented in the learning organization research. Missing from this research are studies focusing on how an organization like the CFD learned from the organizational crisis that began on June 18, 2007, where nine firefighters lost their lives in a furniture warehouse fire, at the individual, team, and organizational levels. This is not the only incident in the history of the fire service where multiple firefighters have lost their lives.

On December 3, 1999, six firefighters perished in a cold storage warehouse fire in Worcester, Massachusetts, on September 11, 2001, hundreds of emergency responders perished following a terrorist attack in New York, and on June 30, 2013, nineteen firefighters perished while battling a wildfire outside of the town of Yarnell, Arizona. Due to the magnitude of these events, these respective departments experienced an organizational crisis similar to the CFD. These three events indicated a need for a scientific study that focused on how an organization like the CFD learned following an organizational crisis due to a line of duty death (LODD) at the individual, team, and organizational levels.

The incident that occurred on June 18, 2007 is of particular significance due to it being the second largest loss of life in the fire service since the two aforementioned incidents in Worcester and New York. Following these events, no study was completed to ascertain how these organizations learned from their multiple LODD incidents at the individual, team, and organizational levels. With the completion of the present study, future organizations that may experience a LODD will have sound research to reference when diagnosing how their department needs to progress toward a learning organization following this type of tragedy.

Therefore, research indicating how the CFD learned from their organizational crisis at these levels offers information to other organizations that may experience an organizational crisis due to a LODD. The continuing failure of organizations to learn from these times of organizational crisis creates political, social, financial, and individual costs that are attributable to the misunderstanding of learning processes (Elliot, 2009). The indication of how the CFD learned from their organizational crisis at the individual, team, and organizational levels can clarify the misunderstanding of these learning processes. They continue to be misunderstood because of the lack of research focusing on different types of organizational crises, and how these organizations learned from their respective failures.

PROBLEM STATEMENT

It was not known how an organization like the CFD learned from an organizational crisis at the individual, team, and organizational levels. This presents a problem because research indicated that under specific conditions, negative impacts stemming from an organizational crisis in one organization could spread to another organization in the same industry (Tieyang et al., 2008). Previous studies regarding NASA and Johnson and Johnson prove that when organizations learn from their crises, they can make the necessary changes to survive. However, even if organizations like the CFD never experience an organizational crisis, this research allows them to be properly prepared if an occurrence similar to that of the CFD is experienced.

Specifically, this study investigated how the CFD, comprised of 318 firefighters that protect approximately 130 square miles, learned from the organizational crisis of the June 18, 2007 incident at the individual, team, and organizational levels. When these unexpected types of crises are encountered by high reliability organizations, such as the fire service, it becomes more difficult for individuals to learn from the unstable, unsafe, and rapidly changing environments that elicit their responses (Baran & Scott, 2010). The results of this study equip such organizations as the CFD with scientific research to learn from such changing environments that create organizational crisis, similar to the one that the CFD experienced following June 18, 2007.

Results from previous research indicated that NASA experienced an organizational crisis following the Challenger disaster (James, 2007). NASA learned from this failure, helping to respond more effectively to the Columbia disaster. However, participant responses indicated that even though NASA learned better response techniques to crises, the organization's capacity to learn was limited by problematic routines and structures (James, 2007). Regardless of this outcome, NASA was able to learn on multiple fronts including transparency, organizational communication, and technology (James, 2007).

According to James (2007), from the time following the Challenger incident, the most evident shift in leadership policy was that of the use of the open door policy, increasing the transparency of the organization. Results also indicated that members of NASA had difficulties with trust, which is problematic for organizational learning (James, 2007). In addition, with NASA's continual movement forward, results indicated that the organization had difficulties allotting the appropriate time to learn from the past. However, even with this lack of time allotted, NASA still indeed learned from previous failures (James, 2007).

Following the terrorist attacks of the World Trade center in 2001, the FDNY experienced an organizational crisis as well. Research indicated that due to communication problems on scene on 9/11, firefighters were not able to effectively communicate with other organizational members, including critical commanders (Taft, 2011). Due to this lack of communication, on scene commanders were unable to discern the status outside of the towers, severely weakening the command structure when the buildings ultimately collapsed and the incident command post was destroyed (Taft, 2011).

A report completed to evaluate the department's response to the 9/11 attacks by McKinsey & Co. indicated that the large response to the disaster taxed the efforts to manage FDNY equipment and personnel in numerous ways (Taft, 2011). From this recommendation, the FDNY created the Fire Department Operations Center (FDOC), which monitors primarily citywide incidents, but has global capabilities as well (Taft, 2011). It offers the department advanced incident command and control, where situational awareness, information, and intelligence can be utilized more adequately than they were on 9/11. Results from studies focusing on this event argued that the steps taken by the FDNY are indicative that they learned from their crisis and responded in a manner that not only provided them with more advanced technology in the event of another disaster, but the global community as well (Taft, 2011).

Another organization that experienced an organizational crisis in the past was Health International Holdings (HIH), documented as one of Australia's largest corporate failures (Cheng & Seeger, 2012). Results of this crisis study indicated that HIH ignored warning signs of financial problems in the beginning phases of the crisis (Cheng & Seeger, 2012). For example, a letter was sent to the chairman of the board of HIH, bringing to light concerns of the amount of material given to the board as well as its relevance and quality. However, the board members stated that the information presented was not sufficient for the board to make decisions (Cheng & Seeger, 2012). This result indicated that even though concerns were raised during the crisis, the organization did not listen or learn from the communication that came from the stakeholders, causing the crisis to grow and destroy a company that had previously been highly successful. This evidence directly related to the current study because, similar to HIH, the CFD did not heed critical recommendations before June 18, 2007.

There is a critical need for organizations such as the CFD facing unstable, unsafe, and rapidly changing environments to learn from the tragic experiences encountered. According to the U.S Fire Administration (2013), 83 firefighters were killed in the line of duty in 2012. This indicated that many different fire service organizations are effected by line of duty deaths (LODD), which can lead to organizational crisis, as evidenced in the CFD from the events that occurred on June 18, 2007. Therefore, if such organizations as the CFD can learn from the CFD's experiences at the individual, team, and organizational levels, then they will be effectively equipped to respond to the unstable, unsafe, and rapidly changing environments with which they are presented. In addition, learning at these levels from the CFD's crisis can reduce the chances of another organization in the same industry suffering negative effects stemming from organizational crisis (Tieyang et al., 2008). When this is considered relative to the NASA and Johnson and Johnson studies that showed how organizations learn from organizational crisis, they will be more adequately equipped to make the necessary changes to survive and the need for this research is apparent.

Through this study, the researcher aimed to discover how the CFD learned from organizational crisis at the individual, team, and organizational levels. Since research indicated that an organizational crisis could spread from one organization to another in the same industry, it is imperative that organizations like the CFD be prepared to combat this in the event of a possible organizational crisis. Furthermore, through this discovery, the researcher offers evidence to other organizations like the CFD to assist them in the identification of areas where they may need to improve to decrease the chances of an organizational crisis.

The researcher's findings solved the problem of not knowing by providing evidence regarding how the CFD learned from an organizational crisis at the individual, team, and organizational levels.

With this research, such organizations as the CFD are able to identify how organizational learning can help organizations incorporate
a specific set of strategies and/or approaches that impact more effective and efficient decision-making in the occurrence of future crises.
This more effective and efficient decision–making may reduce public service fatalities, as well as negative financial impacts for all types
of organizations. The researcher utilized a triangulation of data
sources incorporating Watkins and Marsicks's DLOQ (1997), one-
on-one interviews completed by the researcher, and artifact analysis.

PURPOSE OF THE STUDY

The purpose of this qualitative case study was to indicate how an
organization like the CFD learned from an organizational crisis
at the individual, team, and organizational levels in The City of
Charleston Fire Department in South Carolina following June 18,
2007. Previous studies found evidence that can help organizations
recover and grow from the grave consequences of an organizational
crisis with organizational learning.

At this stage in the research, organizational crisis is generally
defined as a condition that is considered extraordinary, damaging, and disruptive to an organization's state of operations (Snyder
et al., 2006). Although they are high impact events that have a low
probability of occurring, they impose threats on the accountability
and reliability of an organization (Tieyang et al., 2008). According
to Lahteenmaki et al. (2001), the ability of an organization to learn
is a prerequisite for organizational survival and creates a competitive advantage. Organizational learning is defined as a collective

17

learning process where group-based and individual "learning experiences concerning the improvement of organizational performance and/or goals are transferred into organizational routines, processes and structures, which impact the future learning activities of the organizations members" (Schilling & Kluge, 2009, p. 338). Therefore, if organizations do not continuously change internally and adapt to changes met in their operational environment, survival and success will become difficult (Lahteenmaki et al., 2001). If organizational crises are mismanaged or ignored, the sustainability and competitiveness of an organization will be reduced greatly, with both the organization and its stakeholders experiencing the impacts.

The study was conducted through the perceptions of those involved using the lens of organizational learning. With the triangulation of data gathered from incorporating Watkins and Marsick's (1997) DLOQ, interviews, and artifact analysis, the researcher identified how the CFD learned from the June 18, 2007 incident at the individual, team, and organizational levels. Knafl and Breitmayer (1989) indicated that the collection and comparison of triangulated data enhances the quality of the data with idea convergence and the confirmation of the researcher's findings. Additionally, Baxter and Jack (2008) stated that triangulation is a primary strategy that is used in case study research to allow the phenomena to be "viewed and explored from multiple perspectives" (p. 556). From these multiple viewpoints, the CFD, as well as other organizations, can identify how organizational learning helps organizations incorporate a specific set of strategies and/or approaches that impact more effective and efficient decision-making in the occurrence of future crises that they may encounter.

Watkins and Marsick's (1997) DLOQ focused on seven dimensions including continuous learning, inquiry and dialogue, team learning, embedded systems, empowerment, system connection, and strategic leadership. It consisted of the individual level, the team level, and the organizational level. The individual level was measured in questions 1-13, where the focus was upon the dimensions of continuous learning, inquiry, and dialogue. The team level was measured in questions 14-19, where the dimensions of team learning and embedded systems were stressed. Finally, the organizational level was measured from questions 20-55, where empowerment, system connection, and strategic leadership were specified (Watkins & Marsick, 1997).

The following question from the section in the DLOQ measures the individual level: "In my organization, people openly discuss mistakes in order to learn from them" (Marsick & Watkins, 2003, p. 143). Included in the instructions to the participants, the phrase "Do you believe since June 18, 2007" was added as a preface to each question. Therefore, the question read as follows: Do you believe since June 18, 2007, "In my organization, people openly discuss mistakes in order to learn from them?" (Marsick & Watkins, 2003, p. 143). Possible ratings for the above question, as well as the other measurement questions, were 1-6, where 1 was almost never and 6 was almost always. The researcher was granted permission to utilize the DLOQ in this study via electronic mail (Appendix B, on page XXIV).

A purposive sample of these participants was also interviewed, with the researcher asking the following open-ended questions that were created by an expert panel of command level officers, each with over 30 years' of fire experience. The five participants were asked the following open-ended questions:

1. How does the CFD discuss mistakes to allow its members and the fire service to learn from them?
2. How does the CFD utilize committees to support the direction of the department?
3. How does the CFD ensure that all employees are aware of lessons learned from previous emergency and training incidents?
4. How have you learned and improved as a firefighter since June 18, 2007?
5. How has the CFD's leadership changed since June 18, 2007?

The third source of research utilized in the triangulation was the use of artifacts that highlight the CFD since June 18, 2007. These artifacts consisted of newspaper articles, the CFD's Strategic Plan, CFD standard operating procedures, CFD memos, CFD policies, and fire service articles focusing on the CFD's improvements following June 18, 2007. This data source indicated specific areas where the CFD made significant operational, training, and leadership changes.

The specific sample of the population were 27 firefighters that officially responded to the June 18, 2007 incident and were still employed with the CFD at the time of this study. Before June 18, 2007, the CFD was comprised of 246 members, with only 140 of these 246 members remaining with the CFD currently in 2013. Therefore, out of the 318 current employees, 140 of them are from the time period before June 18, 2007. However, all of the 318 employees were affected by this crisis as the department continued to progress through the change process following the incident. The remaining members were all male, ranging in ranks from firefighter to the chief officer level. Ages ranged from 25 to 60 years of age, while experience in the fire service ranged from 1 to 40 years. This is the only information given regarding the characteristics of the remaining members of the CFD that responded to June 18, 2007, as the researcher does not want to give too much information that will allow for the identification of the study's participants.

The expected outcome of the study was to deliver sound scientific research on an event that has not been rigorously researched. Many articles and independent studies were written regarding the practices, equipment, and personnel of the department. However, a scientific study focusing on the responding firefighter's experiences of the event was not completed. These experiences and beliefs from the responding firefighters are important to document how an organization like the CFD learned from an organizational crisis following June 18, 2007 at the individual, team, and organizational levels. This new research enables firefighters to learn from the crisis and become more successful when faced with the possible occurrence of future crises.

RESEARCH QUESTION(S)

The overarching question of this study was as follows: How were organizational processes and employee behaviors changed following a crisis? This overarching question was answered by the guidance of the research questions, which included the following:

R1: How did the CFD learn from organizational crisis at the individual level?

R2: How did the CFD learn from organizational crisis at the team level?

R3: How did the CFD learn from organizational crisis at the organizational level?

These research questions directed the focus of the study with triangulation utilizing the DLOQ, one-on-one interviews, and artifact analysis. First, the DLOQ is a questionnaire that all participants completed with specific instructions to provide evidence for the three research questions, respectively. Included in the instructions to the participants, the phrase, "Do you believe since June 18, 2007 . . ." was added as a preface for each question in the DLOQ. Therefore, the question read as follows: Do you believe since June 18, 2007, "In my organization, people openly discuss mistakes in order to learn from them?" (Marsick & Watkins, 2003, p. 143).

Five of these participants were randomly selected to participate in an interview with the researcher asking the following questions created by an expert panel of command level officers in the fire service where each had over 30 years' of fire service experience. These questions were developed with a focus on the individual, team, and organizational levels of the CFD. The first interview question asked the participants how the CFD discusses mistakes to allow its members and the fire service to learn from them. This question added evidence to support R1. The second question regarding how the CFD utilizes committees to support the direction of the department adds evidence to support R2. The third question referencing how the CFD ensures that all employees are aware of lessons learned from previous emergency and training incidents will contribute supportive evidence to R3. Second, a fourth question asking, how have you learned and improved as a firefighter since June 18, 2007, added more depth to R1. Finally, the question of how the CFD's leadership has changed since June 18, 2007, added greater depth to R3.

The third source of research utilized in the triangulation of data sources was the use of artifact analysis, which highlighted the CFD since June 18, 2007. These artifacts consisted of newspaper articles, the CFD's Strategic Plan, CFD standard operating procedures, CFD memos, CFD policies, and other fire service articles pertaining to the CFD following June 18, 2007. These artifacts indicated specific areas where the CFD has made significant operational, training, and leadership changes. Furthermore, the research presented from these artifacts focused upon the individual, team, and organizational levels to ensure successful correlation between all three sources utilized in the triangulation.

Webb, Campbell, Schwartz, and Sechrest (1966) proposed the idea of the unobtrusive method, one of the earliest references to triangulation. They argued that "once a proposition has been confirmed by two or more independent measurement processes, the uncertainty of its interpretation is greatly reduced. The most persuasive evidence comes through a triangulation of measurement processes" (Webb, et al, 1966, p. 3). In this study, the role of each data source in the triangulation added to the certainty that the data collected was consistent with the researcher's claims. Furthermore, such a rigorous design enhanced the quality of the findings of this research as perceptions from responders were correlated with internal and external artifact data to add to the responder's indications and decrease the chances of bias due to utilizing only internal sources or one source of data collection.

Gathering perceptions from responders of June 18, 2007, of how an organization like the CFD learned from organizational crisis at the individual, team, and organizational levels, provides other organizations with scientific research regarding how they can learn from their own respective organizational crisis in the event that one was to occur. Furthermore, providing evidence of how an organization like the CFD learned from an organizational crisis in this manner offers scientific evidence of examples successfully used by other organizations.

ADVANCING SCIENTIFIC KNOWLEDGE

Previous research found evidence that can help organizations recover and grow from the grave consequences of an organizational crisis through organizational learning. However, a gap in the literature is presented because no studies focusing on the aforementioned have been completed regarding a fire service organization following a multiple line of duty death incident. James' (2007) study on NASA's crisis indicated that the organization learned from their previous lack of transparency following the Challenger disaster. For example, NASA's response following the Columbia tragedy was more open to public inquiry. A few hours after the Columbia tragedy, NASA's leadership stated that they did not know what happened. Following the Challenger disaster, however, the leadership of NASA created a suspicious and closed organizational climate (James, 2007). This overt willingness of the organization's leaders to shift to a more communication friendly environment indicated a substantial lesson learned from the previous organizational crisis following the Challenger disaster (James, 2007).

Another example of organizational learning from an organizational crisis occurred in September 1982 when Johnson and Johnson experienced a devastating event with one of their products (Simola, 2005). This situation progressed to the level of an organizational crisis as a result of seven fatalities that were associated with the ingestion of Extra Strength Tylenol contaminated with cyanide (Boatright, 2000). Public outrage ensued following the incident, which could have meant devastation for Johnson and Johnson if their executives did not act quickly (Simola, 2005).

As a result, Johnson and Johnson issued a nationwide product recall, even though it appeared that the contamination was in one small geographical area. This product recall cost Johnson and Johnson over $100 million; however, it proved to the public that they were committed to the safety of their customers. As a result of this event, a strengthening of public trust was witnessed, as well as a positive impact on market shares and sales (Fink 1986; Siomkos, 1992). This overt willingness on the part of Johnson and Johnson executives to institute a million dollar product recall and revamp their packaging procedures indicated the lessons learned from the crisis, which ensured that the company recovered from the grave consequences of their respective crisis.

Although research indicated that the concept of the learning organization is well established and a frequently studied topic, there is not a generally accepted method to research the growing concept (Davis & Daley, 2008). While a large amount of this research focused on the importance of learning, empirical research is scant in addressing key elements that are required to construct a learning organization (Davis & Daley, 2008). Furthermore, current studies did not outline the possible impact of the individual, team, and organizational elements on a firm's performance, or the assessment approaches to improve these elements (Davis & Daley, 2008). The current study focused upon these three elements in a fire service organization following a multiple LODD to ascertain an organizations' performance following the event, along with the approaches that were taken to ensure organizational improvement.

A study such as this added to the body of knowledge of organizational crisis because fire service organizations are effected by line of duty deaths yearly. According to the U.S Fire Administration (2013), 83 firefighters were killed in the line of duty in 2012. This indicates that many different fire service organizations are effected by line of duty deaths. Furthermore, from the data collected at the individual, team, and organizational levels relating to the CFD, positive results are expected at each level. The expert generated questions were developed focusing on these three important levels to allow for the correlation of the DLOQ responses, as well as the artifact data analysis (Watkins & Marsick, 1997). The artifacts informed the reader of internal and external literature on the CFD and their change process since June 18, 2007. By dissecting each source of data at these three levels, the researcher was able to better organize the findings and present research of greater strength as a result of triangulation.

It is a responsibility of the CFD to learn and subsequently to share what they have learned with other organizations. To compare this to the James' (2007) study on NASA's organizational crisis, Brong (2004) stated "learning from the accident that claimed the Columbia and its crew is an extraordinary responsibility" (p. 39). Therefore, it is an extraordinary responsibility of the CFD to learn from the incident that claimed nine firefighters. In further comparison of James (2007) and Brong (2004), it was stated that the accident confirmed why quality professionals must be placed at decision-making levels in the organization (Brong, 2004). This also became apparent in the CFD after the June 18, 2007 incident where nine firefighters perished.

Furthermore, this research discovered how an organization like the CFD learned from an organizational crisis at the individual, team, and organizational levels. Weick (1988) stated that organizational crisis is unexpected and endangers organizational goals. When these unexpected types of crises are encountered by high reliability organizations such as the fire service, it becomes more difficult for responders to react to the unstable, unsafe, and rapidly changing environments that elicit their responses (Baran & Scott, 2010). Furthermore, when an organization is faced with a crisis, the dynamic of the organization changes due to the extreme amounts of stress placed on organizational leaders, employees, and stakeholders (James, 2007).

The findings of this study contributed to the knowledge and/or practices in the fire service. First, by identifying how an organization like the CFD learned at the individual, team, and organizational levels, other organizations have sound research indicating what may occur following an organizational crisis from a LODD. Furthermore, the current research allows other public service organizations to identify areas where they may be facing the same challenges that the CFD had following June 18, 2007. If other organizations, whether public or private, can learn from the CFD's organizational crisis, improved organizational practices may become apparent.

SIGNIFICANCE OF THE STUDY

Organizations face crises of various kinds, often with grave consequences. Research indicated that crises can be extremely intense, short lived, gradual, and long-term, creating wide spread problems within the organization and its stakeholders (Snyder et al., 2006). With the understanding that organizational crises have a wide array of characteristics, each and every crisis can be seen as unique and undesirable respective to its own specific uniqueness.

However, no matter the circumstances of an organizational crisis, the viewpoint from the affected organization is that of fear and uneasiness, due to not knowing the critical effects that the crisis will have on the organization (Snyder et al., 2006). It was important to study this problem because of the increase in managerial interest and scientific research produced on organizational crisis, even though there was no universal or accepted terminology (Snyder et al., 2006).

Previous studies discovered how to respond to crisis afterwards, indicating that the improvement of organizational malfunctions and an increased knowledge of the external environment were essential to the response. The advantages of the existing body of knowledge regarding organizational malfunctions and the external environment showcased the beginning phases of an organizational crisis. Lin et al. (2006) stated that occasionally organizations are faced with accidentally triggered crises that have costly ramifications if not handled correctly. March and Simon (1958) stated that organizational crises have roots in the external environment. Perrow (1984) expanded upon this research stating that organizational crises also have roots in the malfunctions of an organization.

In support of March and Simon (1958) and Perrow (1984), Pearson and Mitroff (1983) and Staw, Sandelands, and Dutton (1981) argued that crises are predominately caused by internal and external factors, and can result in catastrophic consequences if the right decisions are not made. This literature added to the significance of the current study because the CFD's organizational crisis was rooted in the external environment, as well as in organizational malfunctions apparent pre June 18, 2007, resulting in a catastrophic event. A proper response following an incident of this magnitude would be for the organization to continuously change and adapt to their operational environment to increase survival and success (Lahteenmaki et al., 2001).

The Routley Report (2008), produced by fire service consultants, assisted the CFD with identifying organizational malfunctions. The report stated that "the situation that occurred in Charleston on June 18, 2007 was predictable and the outcome was preventable" (Routley et al., 2008). The aforementioned, along with the numerous recommendations for the CFD to follow national best practices, was a strong indication that the organization did not recognize or mitigate organizational malfunctions, leading to an organizational crisis.

As research indicated, there were crises that pointed to malfunctions in organizations. However, studies also revealed the importance of knowing how to learn from these crises. Jasko, Popovic, and Prokic (2012) stated that the value of knowing how to learn is critical to increasing the survivability of future crisis. NASA utilized learning in their response following the Columbia disaster. If they did not know how to learn, their response following the Columbia disaster would not have been as successful as it was. For example, following the Columbia disaster, NASA told the media and the public that they did not know what happened. Following the Challenger incident, however, the organization created a suspicious, closed environment surrounding the disaster and the organization (James, 2007). This was indicative that knowing how to learn following the Challenger incident allowed them to respond more effectively and survive the future crisis that resulted following the Columbia disaster.

The aforementioned research is important to the current study as it is indicative of the importance of the organization knowing how to learn from an organizational crisis, revealing how they can make the necessary changes to survive a future crisis. However, even if organizations like the CFD never encounter an organizational crisis, this research allows them to properly prepare themselves in the possible occurrence that another organization may experience one. As research indicated, under specific conditions, negative impacts stemming from an organizational crisis in one organization can spread to another organization in the same industry (Tieyang et al., 2008). Therefore, this research can also prevent the spread of organizational crisis in organizations like the CFD.

Significantly, this study resulted in findings that can shed light on how an organization like the CFD learned following a multiple LODD at the individual, team, and organizational levels. These findings will benefit those in the CFD as they specifically identify the progress of the organization since the tragedy of that day in 2007. Furthermore, firefighters around the country will benefit from this research as they will be better prepared to prevent crises from taking place in their respective organization, and if in the unfortunate event one does occur, they will have research indicating how another organization proceeded during a time of crisis.

RATIONALE FOR METHODOLOGY

The method used to conduct this study was a qualitative case study where the researcher focused on phenomena from a specific organization. The researcher utilized triangulation to gather specific data regarding the CFD and its members. Included in the data triangulation were Watkins and Marsick's DLOQ (1997), interviews utilizing five open-ended questions developed by a panel of three command level officers in the fire service that had over 30 years' of experience respectively, as well as artifact analysis.

Stake (2003) suggested that a "case study is defined by interest in individual cases, not by the methods of inquiry used," where the primary criteria for selection is the "opportunity to learn" (p. 134; Stake, 1995, p. 6). However, Yin (2003) stated that the case study researcher is presented a major challenge to ensure quality practice and procedures are utilized to increase rich and valid research. Additionally, the triangulation of data sources is one of the primary strategies that is used and supports the principle in case studies that "the phenomena be viewed and explored from different perspectives" (Baxter & Jack, 2008, p. 556). The collection and comparison of triangulated data enhances the quality of the research with idea convergence and the confirmation of the researcher's findings (Knafl & Breitmayer, 1989).

According to Toloie-Eshlaghy, Chitsaz, Karimian, and Charkh-chi (2011), advantages of qualitative research methods include enabling the study of phenomena of human beings in their natural setting. Furthermore, the main advantage of qualitative research is that it allows phenomena to be grasped from participant views (Toloie-Eshlaghy et al., 2011). This is always neglected when utilizing a quantitative method rather than a qualitative one (Toloie-Eshlaghy et al., 2011). In addition, Baxter and Jack (2008) posited that potential data sources in a qualitative method might incorporate archival records, documentation, physical artifacts, interviews, and participant observation. "Unique in comparison to other qualitative approaches, within case study research, investigators can collect and integrate quantitative survey data, which facilitates reaching a holistic understanding of the phenomenon being studied" (Baxter & Jack, 2008, p. 554). This directly related to the current study due to the utilization of Watkins and Marsick's (1997) DLOQ as a part of the data collection process.

Questionnaires have many advantages that make them a good choice for data collection (Jones, Murphy, Edwards, & James, 2008). They are low cost and there is a minimal amount of training that must be given to the individuals who administer the questionnaires, as well as those who take the questionnaire (Jones et al., 2008). Questionnaires enable a researcher to reach larger participant numbers in a population than is possible with interviews, and they can be delivered electronically, via the web, or by telephone (Jones et al., 2008). Furthermore, the data from the DLOQ (Watkins & Marsick, 1997) specifically identified where the changes exist at the individual, team, and organizational levels.

Palmerino (1999) posited that interviews offer increased value of research and should be considered by researchers more often. Additionally, Jacob and Furgerson (2012) stated that the primary way in which individuals collect other individual's stories and study specific aspects of the human experience is through interviews. They highlight each and every respondent's best thinking and every word spoken by the respondent can be utilized in multiple ways (Palmerino, 1999). The interview data added depth needed to explain the changes identified by the DLOQ (Watkins & Marsick, 1997).

Watkins and Marsick's (1997) DLOQ was utilized to frame the collection of the artifacts and specify the scope of them at the individual, team, and organizational levels. Specifically, these artifacts included newspaper articles, the CFD's Strategic Plan, CFD standard operating procedures, CFD memos, CFD policies, and other fire service journal articles related to the CFD following June 18, 2007. All of this artifact data presented specific examples of changes at all three studied levels of an organization.

This enriched the data from the other two sources as it added perceptions not only from the CFD both internally and externally, but it also ensured that changes were made with no bias due to some of the data being obtained internally. Furthermore, the DLOQ and interviews set the foundation that indicated the changes, with the artifacts brought in to further strengthen the participant's perceptions of the organization (Watkins & Marsick, 1997). This allowed for richer, in-depth qualitative data.

Case studies offer additional advantages as well. As indicated by Marrelli (2007), case studies provide in depth perspectives that can lead to a rich understanding of problems, they can focus on natural or social events, such as a response to a disaster, and the subject can either be an organization, an individual, or any other entity (Marrelli, 2007). Additionally, Feagin, Orum, and Sjoberg (1991) described case studies as a multi-perspectival analysis, meaning that the researchers take into account not only the actors voice and perspectives, but also the interaction between the actors and relevant groups. This is an important point in case study characteristics. A voice is given to the "powerless and voiceless" (Tellis, 1997, p. 1). When studies are presented by sociological investigations on the homeless and powerless, they are done from the "elite" viewpoint (Feagin et al., 1991; Tellis, 1997). In this investigation, a case study approach supported the researcher's purpose and indicated how an organization like the CFD learned from an organizational crisis at the individual, team, and organizational levels.

The advantages indicated specifically address the components of this study. The substantial and specific grounds of participants produced data that added to the body of knowledge of organizational crisis, organizational learning, and influenced practices in the field as organizations now have research that indicated how an organization like the CFD learned from an organizational crisis following a multiple LODD at the individual, team, and organizational levels. This much needed literature expansion aids not only public service organizations to allow for better decision-making, but all types of organizations as well. Additionally, the opportunity to learn from human beings that responded to the incident in their natural setting with interviews, questionnaires, and artifact analysis indicated how the CFD learned at the individual, team, and organizational levels from the incident on June 18, 2007.

Furthermore, by utilizing a questionnaire that solicited data at these three separate levels, the research produced was rich for the development of the body of knowledge of the studied constructs.

NATURE OF THE RESEARCH DESIGN FOR THE STUDY

A case study was selected as it provides in depth perspectives that can lead to a rich understanding of problems, can focus on natural or social events, such as a response to a disaster, and the subject can either be an organization, an individual, or any other entity (Marrelli, 2007). They offer a multi-perspectival analysis, meaning that the researchers take into account not only the actors voice and perspectives, but also the interaction between the actors and relevant groups (Feagin et al., 1991). This is an important point in case study characteristics. A voice is given to the "powerless and voiceless" (Tellis, 1997, p. 1). When studies are presented by sociological investigations on the homeless and powerless, they are done from the "elite" viewpoint (Feagin et al., 1991; Tellis, 1997). Stake (2003) added a "case study is defined by interest in individual cases, not by the methods of inquiry used," where the primary criteria for selection is the "opportunity to learn" (p. 134; Stake, 1995, p. 6).

Data collected included the utilization of a triangulation of the data incorporating Watkins and Marsick's DLOQ (1997), interviews, and artifact analysis. The researcher first electronically mailed the responders a recruitment letter to explain the study (Appendix C, on page XXV). A consent form was also included upon their agreement to participate (Appendix D, on page XXVI). This form stated that the study was confidential and that they were not required to include any personal information. Also, the consent form included language that stated that the participants could withdraw from the study at any time. By triangulating the aforementioned research sources, the researcher identified how the CFD learned at the individual, team, and organizational levels following the crisis.

All participants were electronically mailed a link to Kwiksurveys.com in order to access the DLOQ (Watkins and Marsick, 1997). The participants accessed the link and completed the survey with specific instructions. For example, the following is a question from the section in the DLOQ that measured the individual level: "In my organization, people openly discuss mistakes in order to learn from them" (Marsick & Watkins, 2003, p. 143). Included in the instructions to the participants, the phrase "Do you believe since June 18, 2007 . . ." was added as a preface. Therefore, the question read as follows: Do you believe since June 18, 2007, "In my organization, people openly discuss mistakes in order to learn from them?" (Marsick & Watkins, 2003, p. 143). Possible ratings for the above question, as well as the other measurement questions, were 1-6, where 1 is almost never and 6 is almost always.

The researcher interviewed five of these participants with the following questions created by an expert panel of command level officers, each with over 30 years' of fire service experience. The first question asked the participants, how does the CFD discuss mistakes to allow its members and the fire service to learn from them. Second, how does the CFD utilize committees to support the direction of the department? Third, how does the CFD ensure that all employees are aware of lessons learned from previous emergency and training incidents? Fourth, how have you learned and improved as a fire-fighter since June 18, 2007? Finally, how has the CFD's leadership changed since June 18, 2007?

The third source of data to be utilized in the triangulation was the use of artifacts that highlighted the CFD since June 18, 2007. These artifacts consisted of newspaper articles, the CFD's Strategic Plan, CFD standard operating procedures, CFD memos, CFD policies, and fire service articles relating to the CFD following June 18, 2007. These data sources indicated specific areas where the CFD made significant operational, training, and leadership changes.

Triangulation for this study involved using three sources of data collection for the production of richer and more in-depth scientific research. If the researcher only interviewed the participants, some of the responses may have contained bias, as the researcher was the interviewer. If questionnaires were utilized exclusively, the qualitative nature of the study would not have been as in-depth as it was with the inclusion of interviews. Finally, with the incorporation of artifact analysis, sources indicating the lessons learned from June 18, 2007 added to the participant's claims regarding the direction of the organization since this tragic event.

A qualitative approach was utilized as the study of phenomenon in its natural setting can be studied in greater depth, rather than the testing of theories with the examination of variables. The research design aligned with the selected methodology because of the data that was produced from answers to the DLOQ (Watkins & Marsick, 1997), interviews, and research from artifact analysis. An electronic mail message with an enclosed link and a request for the responder to participate in the study was sent to each participant.

Five participants also participated in a one-on-one interview with the researcher to answer five open-ended questions that were developed by command level officers who each had over 30 years' of fire service experience. Relevant data gathered from the research questions indicated how the CFD learned from an organizational crisis at the individual, team, and organizational levels following June 18, 2007.

Ascertaining how the CFD learned from an organizational crisis in this manner provides other organizations scientific research of how they can learn from their own respective organizational crisis if they were to encounter this experience. Also, identifying how the CFD learned from an organizational crisis at these three levels offers organizations information to help them recognize that they may be currently experiencing, or on the road to experiencing, an organizational crisis. As stated by Brong (2004), relative to NASA's organizational crisis, it is an extraordinary responsibility for the organization to learn from the incident; therefore, it is also an extraordinary responsibility for the CFD to do the same.

Predicted results included a greater understanding of how the CFD learned from an organizational crisis at the individual, team, and organizational levels. Relative to the three research questions, it is expected that the CFD learned from the organizational crisis that ensued post June 18, 2007 at the individual, team, and organizational levels. Furthermore, the predicted results to the research questions provide organizations with scientific evidence of a topic that has not been rigorously researched.

The setting for the research study was in The City of Charleston Fire Department in Charleston, South Carolina. Over 300 firefighters that protect more than 100,000 citizens were specified as the population of interest. Participants involved in the study included 21 firefighters from The City of Charleston Fire Department that responded to the June 18, 2007 incident where nine firefighters perished. The participant sample was selected from firefighters that were still employed with the CFD at the time of this study and whom officially responded to June 18, 2007. The researcher electronically mailed the official responders from June 18, 2007 a recruitment letter explaining the nature of the study (Appendix C, on page XXV). If they agreed to participate, they electronically mailed the researcher back expressing their interest. Following this, the researcher electronically mailed a link to Kwiksurveys.com to complete Watkins and Marsick's (1997) Dimensions of The Learning Organization Questionnaire (DLOQ), which was due by a specific deadline. Five randomly selected participants were then interviewed and the artifact data analysis was then completed.

DEFINITION OF TERMS

The following terms were used operationally in this study:

Crisis. "An unstable or crucial time or state of affairs in which a decisive change is impending: especially one with the distinct possibility of a highly undesirable outcome . . .a situation that has reached a critical phase" (Crisis, n.d.).

The Dimensions of the Learning Organization Questionnaire (DLOQ). A questionnaire developed by Dr. Karen E. Watkins and Dr. Victoria J. Marsick that delves into participants' thoughts relative to how their "organization supports and uses learning at an individual, team, and organizational level" (Watkins & Marsick, 1997, p. 2). From the aforementioned data, the participants and the organization "will be able to identify the strengths that can be built upon and the areas of greatest strategic leverage for development toward becoming a learning organization" (Watkins & Marsick, 1997, p. 2).

National Institute of Standards and Technology (NIST). "A non-regulatory federal agency within the U.S. Department of Commerce. NIST's mission is to promote U.S. innovation and industrial competitiveness by advancing measurement science, standards and technology in ways that enhance economic security and improve our quality of life" (National Institute of Technology, 2012, p. 1).

Occupational Safety and Health Administration (OSHA). "The main federal agency charged with the enforcement of safety and health legislation" (Osha.gov, 2012, p. 1).

Organization. "An administrative and functional structure" (Organization, n.d.). This was reflected in the CFD.

Organizational crisis. "An extraordinary condition that is disruptive and damaging to the existing operating state of an organization" (Snyder et al., 2006, p. 372). This was reflected in the CFD following the incident on June 18, 2007 where nine firefighters perished.

Organizational learning theory. An "organizationally regulated collective learning process in which individual and group-based learning experiences concerning the improvement of organizational performance and/or goals are transferred into organizational routines, processes and structures, which in turn effect the future learning activities of the organizations members" (Schilling & Kluge, 2009, p. 338). Although research indicates that the organizational learning theory and a learning organization have different research dichotomies, Song, Joo, and Chermack (2009) indicated that The Dimensions of the Learning Organization Questionnaire adequately measures a learning organization as a support system for organizational learning. Furthermore, they posited that the DLOQ's theoretical framework includes both concepts of organizational learning and the learning organization (Watkins & Marsick, 1997). To ensure that the instrument was generalizable, it was tested in various cultures including the United States, Taiwan, China, and Colombia (Ellinger, Ellinger, Yang, & Howton, 2002; Hernandez, 2000; Lien, Hung, Yang, & Li, 2006; Yang et al., 2004; Zhang, Zhang, & Yang, 2004).

Organizational malfunction. "A departure from acceptable or desirable practice on the part of a group of individuals that results in unacceptable or undesirable results" (Bea, 2006, p. 3).

ASSUMPTIONS, LIMITATIONS, DELIMITATIONS

The following assumptions were present in this study:

It is assumed that survey participants in this study were not deceptive with their answers, and that the participants answered questions both honestly and to the best of their ability. All participants completed an anonymous questionnaire to ensure open and honest response. When possible participants were approached, a reoccurring concern was anonymity of their questionnaires. The participants stated that they would feel more comfortable and forthright in their responses if the questionnaire were anonymous. However, five of the participants agreed to participate in a one-on-one interview with the researcher to answer five open-ended questions. This method was chosen to ensure that the results would be conducive to developing the body of knowledge of organizational crisis and organization learning in a qualitative manner. It is also assumed that the emotions that remain will not distort the perceptions of the respondent or the accuracy of their answers to the questionnaire or interviews.

It is assumed that this study is an accurate representation of the situation in The City of Charleston Fire Department pre and post June 18, 2007. All of the participants had experience with the organization; therefore, they had significant knowledge of organizational operation. Furthermore, the participants' differing levels of rank and time on the job ensured an accurate representation because all groups' ranks were represented. This element of equity of attention was important, as the results would more likely be reflective of the differing personnel of the department.

The following limitations/delimitations were present in this study:
Lack of funding limited the scope of this study. This study

was produced by a doctoral student who did not have any outside funding. Therefore, the study was operated on a personal budget and could have been expanded upon if there was available funding. If funding were available, the researcher would have included all CFD responders to June 18, 2007. With compensation, it may have been easier to attain a larger number of responders both active and retired.

The survey of firefighters was delimited to only City of Charleston firefighters from one county within South Carolina. Other agencies did respond to the event on June 18, 2007, however, participants did not come from these other agencies. They were not chosen because the study focused on finding scientific research from The City of Charleston Fire Department.

A limitation of the study design consisted of the size of the participant sample. Many of the responders have retired or moved on to other careers, making it difficult to locate them. If a larger participant list could be used, the results would indicate a larger portion of the responders.

Another limitation of the study design was an anonymous questionnaire. This is seen as a positive and a negative for the study. First, the positive was that the participants could be candid in their answers without fear of retaliation. The negative aspect of an anonymous questionnaire was that the participants would not be held accountable for their answers; therefore, they could have put down half-truths or untrue statements that would have changed the dynamic of the research study.

The findings of this study provide guidelines to other organizations that have faced similar crises or have the potential of facing crisis. Furthermore, the DLOQ (Watkins & Marsick, 1997) has been proven to be applicable to many types of organizations and cultural settings. This indicates that the DLOQ (Watkins & Marsick, 1997) is generalizable to many different types of organizations and provides scholarly research for organizational development.

SUMMARY AND ORGANIZATION OF THE REMAINDER OF THE STUDY

Research indicated that the continuing failure of organizations to learn from times of organizational crisis creates political, social, financial, and individual costs that are attributable to the misunderstanding of learning processes (Elliot, 2009). To offer research focusing on an organization that experienced these types of costs, this chapter focused on an overview of organizational crisis and organizational learning, as well as specifics regarding the methodology utilized in the study. This research indicated how an organization like the CFD learned following an organizational crisis at the individual, team, and organizational levels.

Chapter 2 expands on this idea with an extensive review of the literature regarding organizational crisis and organizational learning. Therefore, Chapter 2 presents a review of current research on the centrality of the dissertation literature review in research preparation. Chapter 3 describes the methodology, research design, and procedures for this investigation. Next, Chapter 4 details how the data was analyzed and provides both a written and graphic summary of the results.

Finally, Chapter 5 is an interpretation and discussion of the results as it relates to the existing body of research related to the dissertation topic.

CHAPTER 2
Literature Review

INTRODUCTION TO THE CHAPTER AND BACKGROUND TO THE PROBLEM

The City of Charleston Fire Department (CFD) experienced an organizational crisis after the June 18, 2007 multiple line of duty death (LODD) incident where nine firefighters lost their lives in a furniture warehouse fire. Following this, the organization and its leaders were under scrutiny from many different governing bodies of the fire service. Subsequent investigations performed by these governing bodies, including The Occupational Safety and Health Administration (OSHA) and The National Institute of Standards and Technology (NIST), as well as a study entitled *The Routley Report* (2008), indicated the causal factors that took many lives were outdated equipment and unsafe firefighting techniques. Due to these investigations and the media attention that followed, the department faced an organizational crisis. This crisis was investigated to ascertain how an organization like the CFD learned from the June 18, 2007 incident at the individual, team, and organizational levels.

This is important to the field because fire service organizations experience LODD's yearly. According to the U.S Fire Administration (2013), 83 firefighters were killed in the line of duty in 2012. This indicates that many different fire service organizations are effected by line of duty deaths, which can lead to organizational crisis, as was indicated in the CFD from the events that occurred on June 18, 2007. After a line of duty death, fire service organizations launch investigations to find the cause. Was it a causality of the job or was it a senseless loss of life that could have been prevented with safer techniques? The organization can learn from this incident by identifying the specific areas where the CFD needed improvements to ensure future crises can be proactively prevented or avoided.

To ensure that the CFD hired a leader that was capable of managing and evolving organizational learning, the city embarked on a national search for a new fire chief. Soliman (2011) stated that organizational learning "is a process that involves interactions among individuals and decision makers" (p. 1354). Ortenbald (2004) posited that a learning organization must include organizational learning, on the job learning, an organizational structure that is organic and flexible, and most importantly, a climate of learning. To increase the chances for improvement of the CFD's organizational learning, a new fire chief, Thomas Carr from Montgomery County, Maryland Fire and Rescue Service, was hired. He was described by many as a "firefighter's firefighter", and a "new breed of chief" by Mary Beth Michos, the executive director of the International Association of Fire Chiefs (Bischoff, 2010, p.1).

Organizational learning is significant in situations similar to what the CFD experienced. James' (2007) study was the foundational theoretical basis upon which this study was built. However, the focus of this current study centered directly upon the organizational learning element to ascertain how an organization like the CFD learned from an organizational crisis at the individual, team, and organizational levels. Organizational learning in James' (2007) research was connected to the problem because it is a specific theory that could be utilized during organizational crisis to aid in the development of an organization. James utilized organizational learning to ascertain how NASA learned from previous crises. More specifically, he focused on how the Challenger disaster shaped the organization and their response to future disasters, mainly the Columbia disaster.

James (2007) implemented a qualitative approach, employing triangulation. Interviews with current and past employees of NASA were utilized to attain the results, along with the dissection of the Columbia Action Incident Board Report to address the research questions. Findings indicated that NASA did learn from previous failures, which ensured a better response for the Columbia disaster. The participants, indicating the major role played by leadership during the Columbia tragedy and the responsibility and team direction that was taken by individuals, identified two themes: application of crisis planning and transparency. Finally, respondents indicated that leaders learned from previous failures, including the mishandling of the Challenger incident and assumed responsibility for enhancing NASA's visibility during post-crisis Columbia communication (James, 2007).

According to Schilling and Kluge (2009), the topic of organizational learning was first introduced in 1965. Toulabi, Dehghani, and Reza Al Taha (2012) argued that organizational learning was initially discussed by March et al. (1963). An example of a past study focusing on this theory was conducted by Perkins et al. (2007). Research questions for Perkins' study included the following: "How do nonprofit organizations serve as contexts for individual learning and development?", "What are the key organizational learning characteristics of successful community-based nonprofits?", and "How do nonprofit organizations become effective agents of community change?" (Perkins et al., 2007, p. 309). A three-phase study over a two-year period in a Southern mid-size city was utilized to complete the study. Results indicated that at the individual level, organizations offer opportunities for task relation, role learning, and personal transformative change. Furthermore, the study indicated that organizational change and sustainability are interdependent. To gain sustainability, organizations need to facilitate transformative learning and subsequent change. More importantly, organizations and their employees need to continually learn to adapt to their changing environments (Perkins et al., 2007).

Egan, Yang, and Bartlett (2004) focused on the following research questions: Is employee job satisfaction impacted by organizational learning culture? Are employee's motivation to transfer learning impacted by job satisfaction and organizational learning culture? How are employee's turnover intentions affected by job satisfaction and organizational learning culture? One part of the methodology for this study included The Dimensions of Learning Organization Questionnaire (DLOQ) (Watkins & Marsick, 1997), which measured organizational learning culture. Results indicated that organizational learning culture has significant positive contributions on motivation to transfer learning and job satisfaction (Egan et al., 2004).

Lynn et al. (1997) also focused on the topic of organizational learning. The researchers asked if a model of organizational learning derived from information-processed constructs could be formulated, and if this model was found, how it affected the new product success rate. The methodology included the use of questionnaires to gather the data about new product information retrieving, reviewing, and recording practices, with financial performance, new product performance, as well as research and development expenditure statistics. Results indicated that organizational learning has a positive impact on new product success and new product success is affected by the improvement of researching and tracking previous designs of products, and the reaction the market sustained from these designs (Lynn et al., 1997).

The development of the organizational learning theory has increased since its inception in the 1960s, with even more increased interest being received from practitioners and researchers over the past two decades (Crossan et al., 1999). Resulting from this increased interest, Watkins and Marsick (1997) created The Dimensions of the Learning Organization Questionnaire (DLOQ). This resulting instrument utilizes seven specific and interrelated action imperatives including the creation of continuous learning opportunities, the promotion of inquiry and dialogue, the encouragement of collaboration and team learning, the establishment of systems to capture and share learning, the empowerment of people toward a collective vision, the connection of the organization to its environment, and the provision of strategic leadership for learning (Davis & Daley, 2008).

This survey was utilized in the study conducted by Egan et al. (2004), where they utilized the DLOQ (Watkins & Marsick, 1997) to measure organizational learning culture. Key findings indicated that organizational learning culture has significant positive contributions on motivation to transfer learning and job satisfaction (Egan et al., 2004). Sahaya (2012) also utilized the DLOQ (Watkins & Marsick, 1997) in a study. Key findings suggested that the firms that were studied had specific elements of a learning organization, which include the empowerment of people and the providing of strategic leadership for learning (Sahaya, 2012).

There were also other approaches used to study organizational learning. For example, in Perkins et al. (2007), a three-phase study was utilized in a two-year period without the use of the DLOQ (Watkins & Marsick, 1997). Interviews with open-ended questions utilizing a semi-structured format focusing on organizational crisis and organizational goals were used. The interviews were recorded, transcribed, and placed into NVivo, a coding software program for qualitative data (Perkins et al., 2007).

Comparatively, in their work on organizational learning, Lynn et al. (1997) also utilized a questionnaire other than the DLOQ (Watkins & Marsick, 1997). These questionnaires were used to gather the data about new product information retrieving, reviewing, and recording practices, with financial performance, new product performance, as well as research and development expenditure statistics. The items included in the measurement were developed from the literature and confirmed in interviews with firms participating in the study (Lynn et al., 1997).

There was existing literature on organizational crisis that related to organizational learning. The researcher located this literature by utilizing Grand Canyon University's (GCU) online library and the Charleston County, South Carolina (SC) public library system. Specifically, databases utilized from GCU's online library focusing upon peer-reviewed articles included Academic Search Complete, ProQuest Central, and OmniFile Full Text Select. The researcher utilized the following terms to search the databases: organizational crisis, organizational learning, fire service line of duty death (LODD) incidents, military crises, organizational resilience, organizational behavior, and organizational leadership and development. Comparatively, the Charleston County, SC public library system was utilized to locate authors' work's that were found in the GCU online library database. This allowed the researcher to expand from online databases that included articles from selected authors to specific books that were of interest to expanding the research of this study.

In order to survey and summarize the existing body of knowledge, the researcher compared and contrasted numerous studies on both theories, as this allowed for a more rich synthesis of the current literature. Gaps were identified in the literature of organizational crisis and organizational learning pertaining to a fire service organization following an organizational crisis that stemmed from a multiple LODD. This study fills the gap as it offers sound scientific research to other fire service organizations on what to expect if they are to experience an organizational crisis stemming from a LODD. If they were never to undergo such an experience, they would have information upon which to rely when diagnosing if their organization is on a similar path as the CFD was before June 18, 2007.

The theoretical foundations of this study are presented next, with an exhaustive review of the literature to follow. Specific themes such as organizational crisis and organizational learning were the focus. Furthermore, the identification of sub-themes were also identified with the selection of three current studies focusing on that respective sub-theme. Following the sub-theme presentation, the three respective studies were synthesized to identify their similarities and differences. Chapter 2 closes with a summary of the literature review and an outline of the information included in Chapter 3.

THEORETICAL FOUNDATIONS

Argyris (2002) indicated that the organizational learning theory is divided into two distinct areas, including both single and double loop learning. Single loop learning is defined as correcting errors without changing underlying governing values, while double loop learning is described as a process to correct errors by altering the governing values and actions (Argyris, 2002). Considering this, Yang et al. (2004) posited that organizational learning and the learning organization are "two related yet distinct constructs" that have their differences (p. 34).

The learning organization construct usually pertains to organizations that display continuous learning and adaptive characteristics, or are attempting to institute them. In contrast, organizational learning identifies collective learning experiences utilized to develop skills and attain knowledge (Yang et al., 2004). It can be argued that in order to institute and display continuous learning and adaptive characteristics, collective learning experiences must be first identified to attain the prerequisite knowledge and skills. Therefore, for the purpose of this study, the completion of the DLOQ (Watkins & Marsick, 1997) allowed the CFD to indicate areas at the individual, team, and organizational levels where learning took place. This survey was corroborated with participant interviews and artifact analysis to indicate how the CFD displayed continuous learning and adaptive characteristics from their collective learning experiences since June 18, 2007.

The foundational theoretical model for this study was the seminal work of Watkins and Marsick (1997) with their development of the DLOQ. The components in the DLOQ (Watkins & Marsick, 1997) model consist of seven specific dimensions including continuous learning, inquiry and dialogue, team learning, embedded systems, empowerment, system connection, and strategic leadership. Continuous learning incorporates ongoing education and a work environment designed to allow people to learn on the job. Inquiry and dialogue encourage personnel to ask questions, listen, and express their views to increase their productive reasoning skills. Team learning includes a culture that encourages collaboration, where personnel are expected to and rewarded for doing so. The embedded systems dimension identifies specific systems that must be created, maintained, and integrated into work in order to share learning. Empowerment consists of allowing people to create and institute a shared vision, where the responsibility is dispersed so that people learn what they will be held accountable for. System connection ensures that the organization is linked to the community and that people understand the big picture of how their work effects the entire organization. The strategic leadership dimension incorporates leadership for strategic learning and has leaders not only exemplify learning, but support it as well.

Research Questions 1, 2, and 3 were answered with the above-mentioned DLOQ (Watkins & Marsick, 1997), which all sampled participants completed. The instructions were modified to include the phrase "Do you believe since June 18, 2007" as a preface for each question in the DLOQ. Therefore, the question read as follows: "Do you believe since June 18, 2007, in my organization, people openly discuss mistakes in order to learn from them?"

Five of these participants were chosen to participate in an interview with the researcher asking five open-ended questions created by an expert panel of command level officers in the fire service where each had over 30 years' of fire service experience. The questions are tied to the theory as the expert panel utilized the three levels of the DLOQ (Watkins & Marsick, 1997) to guide the development of the interview questions. This ensured that the questions were grounded in the model of the DLOQ (Watkins & Marsick, 1997) and the answers to the interview questions were able to be correlated with the DLOQ responses. Furthermore, these questions provided rich evidence for R1, R2, and R3 as well.

Artifact analysis then highlighted the CFD since June 18, 2007 with artifacts consisting of newspaper articles, the CFD's Strategic Plan, CFD standard operating procedures, CFD memos, CFD policies, and other fire service articles pertaining to the CFD following June 18, 2007. The study of the artifacts was guided by the DLOQ (Watkins & Marsick, 1997) model at the individual, team, and organizational levels to ensure successful completion of the triangulation utilized in the current study. This data indicated specific areas where the CFD made significant operational, training, and leadership changes, providing even more evidence for the three specified research questions.

A case study by James (2007) supported the development of the study. However, the current study was different than the aforementioned as this study focused specifically on learning following a multiple line of duty death in the fire service. James focused on two incidents that occurred in NASA where members perished. Furthermore, the current study utilized triangulation that incorporated the DLOQ (Watkins & Marsick, 1997), interviews, and artifact data analysis; whereas James did not utilize the DLOQ (Watkins & Marsick, 1997) in the data collection. Specifically, the current study focused on the organizational learning component from the individual, team, and organizational levels, excluding the sense-making element incorporated in James that related specifically to the action taken upon that organizational learning. The key perceptions identified in the study consist of how an organization like the CFD learned after June 18, 2007 at the individual, team, and organizational levels.

Previous studies were completed on organizational learning with qualitative models in for-profit organizations, as well as NASA (James, 2007; Yeo, 2007). The settings for these studies included NASA in James and a large manufacturing firm in Singapore in Yeo. James focused on how NASA learned following the Columbia and Challenger incidents, and Yeo focused on factors that were indicative of organizational learning and effectiveness. However, none has investigated how organizational learning can identify what was learned from an organizational crisis such as a multiple LODD in the fire service, which may in turn help improve responses to future crisis. It is important to investigate and share with other fire service agencies how the CFD learned from the crisis to ensure a tragedy such as this is mitigated in the future of the fire service. Current research on the Columbia disaster indicated that "learning from the accident that claimed the Columbia and its crew is an extraordinary responsibility" (Brong, 2004, p. 39). Therefore, it is an extraordinary responsibility of the CFD to learn from the incident that claimed the lives of nine firefighters.

According to Coldwell, Joosub, and Papageorgiou (2012), an organizational crisis reveals an organizations management's capability to handle this type of negative event. During a critical occurrence, an organization must ensure that effective strategies and resources are utilized to handle the situation efficiently to minimize damage to public trust. If the organization does not do so, then the media will expose it to organizational stakeholders. Comparatively, if the crisis is handled responsibly and successfully by the organization, the organization may enhance specific products or services, as well as their reputation (Coldwell et al., 2012; Senge, 1990). This would indicate substantial organizational learning as the organization would progress from a negative event to a positive learning environment that focused on the enhancement of products or services as a result of lessons witnessed from previous occurrences.

These events also impose a need for organizations to provide strategic leadership for learning, empower people toward a collective vision, create systems to capture and share learning, encourage collaboration and team learning, promote inquiry and dialogue, create continuous learning opportunities, and transform the organization so that it can prevent or improve responses to future crisis (Watkins & Marsick, 1997). Comparatively, other learning theories include Kolb's (1984) experiential learning theory (ELT) that focused on physiology, psychology, and philosophy, as well as Senge's (1990) adaptive and generative learning theory, through the utilization of mental models as an integral component, and Nevis, DiBella, and

Goulds' (1995) assimilation theory that incorporated three unique stages in the learning process. These stages include knowledge acquisition, knowledge sharing, and knowledge utilization (Leavitt, 2011).

This study was grounded in the organizational learning theory. Data were collected which identified, measured, and described how an organization like the CFD learned from an organizational crisis that ensued post June 18, 2007 at the individual, team, and organizational levels. The three aforementioned theories developed by Kolb (1984), Senge (1990), and Nevis et al. (1995) are an important part of the organizational learning literature. However, for this study, they were not specifically targeted as the researcher aimed to complete research that added to a more global perspective of organizational learning, rather than to address one of the specific theories mentioned. Furthermore, the results added to the body of knowledge of organizational crisis and organizational learning with an innovative approach.

REVIEW OF THE LITERATURE

The City of Charleston Fire Department was in despair and disarray after nine firefighters perished in a furniture warehouse fire on June 18, 2007. The department and its leaders were under scrutiny from many different governing bodies of the fire service. These governing bodies completed numerous investigations on the tragedy to aid in the understanding of what took place during the incident. With the investigations, extensive media attention, and calls for the resignation of the command staff, the department experienced an organizational crisis. This crisis was investigated to ascertain how June 18,

2007 caused a department enriched in tradition to change its organizational development and become a progressive department for others to model.

This investigation was important to the field because fire service organizations experience LODD's yearly. After a line of duty death, fire service organizations launch investigations to determine the cause. Was it a causality of the job, or was it a senseless loss of life that could have been prevented with safer techniques? These are difficult questions for leaders to answer. However, investigation to seek answers will create a better understanding of what needs to be implemented to prevent future occurrences. After a LODD, fire service organizations institute new guidelines that refer to the incident in question as a result of the evidence produced in the investigation. A trend developed in the past that indicated fire service organizations were reactive instead of proactive.

The literature review below includes two themes: organizational crisis and organizational learning. Regarding organizational crisis, the subthemes focused upon are related to organizational crisis leadership and planning. Comparatively, the subtheme of organizational learning below directly focuses upon employee learning and development.

ORGANIZATIONAL CRISIS

Snyder et al. (2006) stated that an organizational crisis is a condition that is considered extraordinary, damaging, and disruptive to an organization's state of operations. Although they are high impact events that have a low probability of occurring, they impose threats on the accountability and reliability of an organization (Tieyang et al., 2008). An organizational crisis is characterized by "ambiguity of cause, effect, and means of resolution" (Tieyang et al., 2008, p. 452). Under specific conditions, negative impacts stemming from an organizational crisis in one organization can spread to another organization in the same industry (Tieyang et al., 2008).

Research indicated that the causes of organizational crisis relate to organizational structure and malfunctions, and that many organizations have faced or will face crises that lead to grave consequences. Lin et al. (2006) stated that organizational crises are becoming more inevitable due to the increase of complexity and technology-based processes in organizations. Furthermore, organizations are presented with accident-triggered and technology-based crises that result in disasters if not properly handled (Lin et al., 2006). Perrow (1984) and Rochlin (1991) indicated that crises are bound to take place more specifically in large, complex systems. These crises predominantly stem from the external environment and organizational malfunctions (Perrow, 1984).

Previous studies found evidence that can help organizations recover and grow from the grave consequences of an organizational crisis with learning. James' (2007) study on NASA's crisis indicated that the organization learned from their previous lack of transparency following the Challenger disaster. This gave them the knowledge to combat a future organizational crisis following the Columbia disaster.

Another example of how organizational crisis was handled in the past dates back to September 1982 when Johnson and Johnson experienced a devastating event with one of their products (Simola, 2005).

Boatright (2000) indicated that this devastating event turned into an organizational crisis because of the seven deaths that were associated with the ingestion of Extra Strength Tylenol contaminated with cyanide. This crisis caused public outrage that could have been life-threatening to the Tylenol brand if executives did not do something quickly (Simola, 2005). Collins and Porras (2000) stated that Johnson and Johnson issued a nationwide product recall quickly, even though the contamination seemed to be in one small geographical area. This product recall cost Johnson and Johnson over $100 million dollars and proved to the public that they were committed to the safety of their customers. This resulted in a strengthening of public trust, as well as positively impacting market shares and sales (Fink 1986; Siomkos, 1992).

The effects and consequences of organizational crisis are substantial. For example, critical information was not known, resulting in failure on the part of some organizations in managing their own crises effectively. This was exemplified in the Haitian government's response to the Earthquake that struck Haiti in 2010. As stated by Piotrowski (2010), the Earthquake in Haiti created a crisis of critical and immediate needs for the afflicted population. However, due to turf wars and interagency conflict, the appropriate actions were not taken by the organizations tasked with filling these needs (Piotrowski, 2010).

Another example predating the above event was the response to Hurricane Katrina in 2005. Farazmand (2007) revealed such a response to be a major failure that created a large-scale mismanagement and leadership crisis. These crises could have been managed more effectively if a coordinated planning structure and effective organizational management atmosphere were created where command had certain responsibilities based on priority and an appropriate timeframe (Dynes, 1970; Piotrowski, 2010). These plans may assist in managing crises effectively, however, as the Katrina and Haitian Earthquake events prove, if the plans are not in place and ready for implementation well preceding the crisis, then an organization will not be able to learn and manage their own crisis effectively (Piotrowski, 2010).

Learning from organizational crisis is imperative for the future benefit of organizations. Larson et al. (1998) posited that increased levels of inter-organizational learning are possible with cultures that are more open. This type of open culture specifically benefits planning for future crisis. As the organization plans for future crisis, organizational learning will be an integral part, as the organization will rely on its respective lessons learned, as well as lessons learned from other organizations that may have experienced a similar event.

An example of organizational learning from an organizational crisis in action comes from James (2007), where he indicated that NASA's response following the Columbia tragedy was much more effective than their response following the Challenger incident. Specifically, a few hours after the Columbia tragedy, NASA's leadership stated that they did not know what happened, which reflected the learning of a substantial lesson following the Challenger explosion when NASA's leadership created a suspicious and closed organizational climate (James, 2007). This overt willingness of the organizations leaders to shift to a more communication friendly environment assisted in crisis management following the disaster, resulting in reflection on the part of NASA's leadership that opened to a greater understanding of the value of transparency as they evaluated previous errors (James, 2007). Additionally, this increased media and public support for the organization, with organizational members being allowed to express their opinions throughout the crisis stages following the Columbia disaster (James, 2007).

LEADERSHIP AND PLANNING

Historically, European societal populations were heterogeneous in gender, age, ethnicity, and income with long-standing ethnic diversity that has increased as a result of immigration over the past few decades; highlighting this status to an even greater extent (James, Hawkins, & Rowel, 2007; Olofsson, 2011; Quinn, 2008; Sikisch, 1995; Smith, 1990). A challenge is presented in contingency planning and policy making as both are based on the idea that societies are homogeneous. As a result, the development of custom crisis communication and contingency planning in heterogeneous populations is critical while preparing for crisis. Reaching the target population during emergencies and preventive work are two important areas of contingency planning (James, Hawkins, & Rowel, 2007; Olofsson, 2011; Quinn, 2008; Sikisch, 1995; Smith, 1990). Therefore, contingency planning must be adapted to the present situation and the population that will be affected as well (Olofsson, 2011).

This study increased the body of knowledge of organizational crisis preparedness. It provides a foundation for other organizations to prepare for and understand organizational crisis referring to informal and formal management, as well general circumstance adaptation. The model offers other organizations the tools to develop their own contingency planning to combat organizational crisis, while also posing to government entities a standard measure with which to manage heterogeneity during crisis situations. The purpose of Olofsson's (2011) study was to develop a model of crisis preparedness of organizations in heterogeneous societies and to scientifically investigate the natural element of Swedish municipalities. As part of the model, the natural element was comprised of informal organizational processes and practices, viewed as the opposite of formal planning (Olofsson, 2011).

The aim of Olofsson's (2011) empirical study was to evaluate natural aspects of the Organizational Crisis Preparedness in Heterogeneous Societies (OCPH) model to indicate whether the model was more than a theoretical construct. The study was completed with another research project focusing on formal crisis preparedness in 160 Swedish municipalities, which, according to Olofsson (2007), is 55% of all municipalities in Sweden. By utilizing a previous study, it was possible to identify organizations suitable for investigation. For this study, heterogeneity was defined as ethnicity, even though the OCPH model could possibly embrace gender, age, or disability (Olofsson, 2011).

Olofsson (2011) used a qualitative approach to identify action demanded by the informal factors of open and closed natural crisis preparedness. Risk communicators and crisis managers were interviewed in six municipalities in Sweden. Municipalities were chosen as a result of their assistance with County Administrative Boards in securing their respective geographical area and ensuring the safety of its population. To avoid a situation where interviewed organizations did not focus on ethnicity, the choice of municipality was given

to the six organizations that included ethnicity in formal crisis preparedness in the previous study (Olofsson, 2011).

The interviews were completed with eight people from six different municipalities. Two city districts in the cities of Stockholm
and Gothenburg participated, as well as four small-medium sized
municipalities (Olofsson, 2011). Three interviews were conducted by
telephone and four were conducted in person (Olofsson, 2011). The
municipalities selected to participate varied according to the size of
the population and individuals with foreign backgrounds who had
experiences with previous crises where foreign background individuals were involved. The six selected city districts and municipalities had differing proportions of foreign background individuals
experiencing crises. However, all participants had some experience
of crisis, either inter-organizational or outside of their organization
(Olofsson, 2011).

Each individual interview was approximately one hour in dura-
tion, except for one interview done by telephone that lasted 30 minutes (Olofsson, 2011). The interviews were recorded and analyzed
utilizing qualitative content analysis. Themes were already defined
in the OCPH model, providing for the use of structured coding. The
interviews were then reanalyzed to identify relations of different
concepts, arguments, and how according to municipality, the themes
varied. Quotations were utilized from the interviews because this
type of in-depth analysis can be open to bias and subjective interpretations (Olofsson, 2011).

Results of Olofsson's (2011) study indicated that the OCPH model
emphasizes that there was not a close relationship between informal
and formal crisis preparedness. Furthermore, an organization with

a structured, formalized method of crisis preparedness may not utilize informal practices. With the completion of the study focusing on openness and rationality, the OCPH model showed promise to be useful in categorizing and understanding organizational crisis preparedness. From the basis of the findings of this empirical study, organizations can make the decision to change or develop their crisis preparedness aspects further. This type of analysis assists crisis managers and interested parties in the understanding and improvement of organizational crisis preparedness (Olofsson, 2011).

MEASURING RESILIENCE POTENTIAL: AN ADAPTIVE STRATEGY FOR ORGANIZATIONAL CRISIS PLANNING

Questions existed whether there is a causal relationship between effective response to crisis and predisaster planning (Tierney, Lindell, & Perry, 2001; Wenger, Quarantelli, & Dynes, 1986). Clark (1999) indicated that although success and planning do not coincide, they may have slight connections. Weick and Sutcliffe (2001) posited that having a preconceived plan to respond to hazards discourages organizations in their recognition and response to the unique challenges of events. Instead of viewing plans as the outcome of the processes, a more productive approach might be to consider whether specific elements of planning lead to effective response through the development of the organization. With the realization of organizational resilience potential, adaptive behaviors are enabled along with the use of creativity and improvisation (Somers, 2009).

In organizational research, resilience was defined as an organization's ability to recuperate from a specific event that creates uncertainty and requires an abnormal response (Lengnick-Hall & Beck, 2003; Somers, 2009; Wildavsky, 1988). Furthermore, Sutcliffe and Vogus (2003) described organizational resilience as the skill in managing change or a strain with minimal interruption. Resilience, in its simplest form, is a reaction to a crisis (Lengnick-Hall, & Beck, 2003; Somers, 2009).

The departments of public works agencies in Oklahoma, Texas, Arizona, and New Mexico were used as the analysis units for Somers' (2009) research study. This is a vital department for supplying water for consumption, as well as fire suppression activities. Furthermore, this department was a key supporter of a community's disaster response and crisis management (Somers, 2009). It is extremely important that these public works departments are capable of not only the everyday needs of the community, but in the response to disasters that may cause crises (Anthony, 1994; Cooke, 1994; Wolensky & Wolensky, 1991).

The purpose of Somers' (2009) study was to examine the possibility of creating a technique or tool to measure organizational resilience. Questionnaires were mailed to 142 municipal public works departments, with 96 of them being returned. A senior manager or public works director completed the questionnaire acting as an informant regarding departmental actions. This level of employee was selected to ensure that employees with experience participated and that the completion of the questionnaire was based on the entire scope of the organization, which may have presented a positive bias due to research that suggested that senior management may estimate their resilience higher than other employees (Somers, 2009).

Six factors created by Mallak (1998) were utilized to measure organizational resilience, including the following: risk avoidance, goal directed solution seeking, the understanding of critical situations, solution seeking based on goal direction, reliance on sources of information, resource access, and the ability of organizational members to fill different roles. A single question was developed for each one of the measurement factors, with respondents rating the questions on a visual analog scale (VAS) (Somers, 2009). Also utilized were four questions to identify correlations with organizational resilience and the perception of risk, community planning involvement, accreditation, and organizational structure. Compliance of continuity of operations planning, or COOP, was measured to identify planning progress from the beginning of a plan to a plan's completion. These plans must have been disseminated to the organization and practically utilized in a disaster drill to be included in the measurement (Somers, 2009).

Results from Somers' (2009) study indicated that the Organizational Reliance Potential Survey (ORPS) is an acceptable tool to measure organizations' reliance potential. Furthermore, the results from the surveys indicated that the represented public works departments have differing levels of reliance potential. Managers that felt that a disaster was likely or highly likely had higher scores on the ORPS, however, these scores did not meet an acceptable level of statistical significance.

More significantly, results from Somers' (2009) study supported the three major hypotheses. Individual's behavior motivates others to take protective action regarding risk, and when individuals take these effective actions, risk perception decreases and risk perception reflects risk behavior. Therefore, perceived risk at high levels relates to early planning stages. Finally, results indicated that developing a COOP document only requires the gathering of information by an individual, whereas resilience development is much more complex and necessitates increased ability to identify and understand information from changing environments (Somers, 2009).

RESPONSIBLE LEADERSHIP IN ORGANIZATIONAL CRISIS: AN ANALYSIS OF THE EFFECTS OF PUBLIC PERCEPTIONS OF SELECTED SOUTH AFRICAN BUSINESS ORGANIZATIONS' REPUTATIONS

There was much research produced regarding the similarities and differences between management and leadership (Daft, 1999). For this research study, completed by Coldwell et al. (2012), responsible management was viewed as similar to responsible leadership (Paine, 1994). Other research indicated that responsible management is more critical in organizational ethical conduct because this level of management comprises the largest amount of everyday decision makers (Coldwell et al., 2012). Responsible leadership was defined as building relationships ethically and morally with organizational stakeholders (Coldwell et al., 2012; Maak & Pless, 2006).

Previous research completed by Coldwell et al. (2012) indicated that no research has been done regarding the relationships between crisis, management intervention, corporate reputation, and price values. However, research completed by Accenture (2011) in the United Kingdom and the United States indicated that quality and speed of organizational response to crisis events positively affected corporate reputation and share price values (as cited in Coldwell et al., 2012).

A crisis situation indicates how well an organization can actually deliver effective and responsible actions to mitigate the crisis. If members of the organization are not capable of doing so, media outlets will identify this and disseminate this information to concerned stakeholders. Comparatively, if the organization is able to manage the crisis effectively, this will be indicated in an enhancement of their reputation and share price values. Coldwell's (2012) study suggested a plan to incorporate "a stepwise ideal type model" with specific steps to be put into place preceding and following a crisis (Coldwell et al., 2012, p. 134). This type of approach and its appropriated steps aimed to provide managers with a "responsibility compass" for ethical decision-making during crisis situations (Coldwell et al., 2012, p. 134).

The purpose of Coldwell's (2012) study was to explore the steps taken both before and after the crisis in South African companies in comparison to a "responsibility compass" model on share price resolution and share prices (p. 134). Furthermore, the researchers aimed to explore reputation capital effects, established by responsible managers, on resolution speed and share price decrease following crisis. In order to achieve this, South African companies with crisis experience were utilized to test post crisis share prices against the proposed model's efficacy. Perceptions from specific South African companies regarding brand strength and reputation were gained from accounting students and staff. This was then utilized to evaluate reputation capital effects in the mitigation of crisis-inflicted damage (Coldwell et al., 2012).

The methodology utilized for Coldwell's (2012) research included both a qualitative case study and a quantitative questionnaire.

Two different methods were utilized for the qualitative case study, including documentation and archival sources. Observations and interviews were not utilized because of the time frame of the study. A questionnaire was developed for the quantitative portion of the study, which measured brand strength and corporate reputation in relation to corporate capital. A sample of 117 students and staff from the University of Witwatersrand in South Africa were utilized in the study and were chosen as a convenience sample due to their familiarity of the 10 South African companies' that were selected. These specific 10 companies were chosen due to their firsthand experience with crisis (Coldwell et al., 2012).

The qualitative case study analysis indicated that the speed of implementation of the responsibility compass had an effect on "individual company share prices" (Coldwell et al., 2012, p. 142). The analyzed case studies were in line with Klann's (2003) Level 1 type of crisis and did not include either crisis Levels 2 or 3, which focus on personal injury and loss of life, respectively. The quantitative measurement focusing on corporate reputation and brand strength indicated a slight relationship between the selected company's reputation capital and the effects reputation capital had on resolution of share prices following a crisis (Coldwell et al., 2012).

The correlation analysis indicated that the more steps the company takes to conform with the model and the speed of step implementation, the less the average share prices fall following a crisis (Coldwell et al., 2012). Furthermore, the buildup of reputation with responsible managers has a "buffering effect" (Coldwell et al., 2012, p. 142). The aforementioned findings were consistent with the findings of Fombrun and Van Riel (2004), which indicated reputation capital importance in supporting the reputations of organizations following crisis.

SYNTHESIS OF THE LITERATURE

Leading and planning during organizational crisis situations are essential for organizational resilience and survivability. Research indicated that there was a challenge in planning for these times of crisis (Olofsson, 2011). Furthermore, current studies have attempted to answer specific questions relating to whether there is a causal relationship to predisaster planning and response effectiveness. Olofsson (2011) stated that the development of custom crisis communication and contingency planning is critical while preparing for crisis. In comparison, Weick and Sutcliffe (2001) suggested that having a preconceived plan to respond to hazards discourages organizations in their recognition and response to the unique challenges of events. When management and leadership are added into this equation of crisis planning, the equation becomes even more complicated.

Similarities and differences were present in the purpose of studies that related to organizational crisis. First, Olofsson (2011) aimed to evaluate natural aspects of the Organizational Crisis Preparedness in Heterogeneous Societies (OCPH) model to indicate whether the model was only a theoretical construct or something more. In comparison, Somers (2009) aimed to examine if it was possible to create a tool to measure a specific theory; organizational resilience. Therefore, Olofsson focused on developing the theoretical construct of a specific theory, while Somers addressed developing a measuring tool or technique of a specific theory.

A similarity was identified between the purposes of the three studies regarding organizational crisis preparedness. For example, Olofsson (2011) considered a theory relating to organizational crisis preparedness, while Somers (2009) focused on a theory that assisted organizations in resilience to these types of crises. By attempting to identify organizational resilience and a tool to measure this theory, Somers also sought to identify a method to prepare and respond to a crisis situation. The purpose of Coldwell et al. (2012) was similar to Olofsson and Somers in that they identified pre and post crisis steps, which was similar to crisis planning in Olofsson and organizational resilience in Somers. If an organization learns how to become resilient, they are essentially preparing for the event of a crisis.

The samples of the three examined studies presented differences with Olofsson (2011) utilizing six municipalities in Sweden, Somers (2009) utilizing 142 public works departments in Oklahoma, Texas, Arizona, and New Mexico, and Coldwell et al. (2012) utilizing 117 staff and students from the University of Witwatersrand in South Africa. The participants in the study of Olofsson (2011) and Somers (2009) were similar because they used managerial level participants to attain their data, whereas Coldwell et al. (2012) utilized staff and students. The staff was viewed as a classroom manager; however, the students were not viewed in this light due to their position as learners.

A convenience sample was utilized in Coldwell et al. (2012), whereas, Olofsson (2011) and Somers (2009) targeted a purposive sample. Reasoning for the selection of the participants varied in the studies as well. Olofsson chose municipalities as they were responsible for the security of their geographical area and the safety of its population. Somers chose public works departments because of their requirement to function in an effective manner daily, as well as when crisis strikes. Comparatively, Coldwell et al. chose their participants based on their firsthand experience with crisis situations. Therefore, all three participant samples were chosen differently based on each researcher's specific criterion.

The methodologies utilized in the three studies presented similarities and differences as well. Olofsson (2011) and Somers (2009) utilized only a qualitative approach, while Coldwell et al. (2012) utilized a qualitative case study and a quantitative questionnaire. Olofsson utilized interviews, whereas Somers utilized a questionnaire to gain participant perceptions. In comparison to these two studies, Coldwell et al. included documentation and archival sources for their qualitative data, while using a questionnaire for the quantitative portion of the study. Olofsson's participants completed interviews that lasted up to an hour, whereas Somers' participants completed a questionnaire that was mailed to them. The participants of the study by Coldwell et al. completed a questionnaire, however, the questionnaire in the latter study was utilized to attain quantitative data rather than qualitative, as Somers did.

Olofsson's (2011) findings indicated that the OCPH model emphasizes that there is not a close relationship between informal and formal crisis preparedness. In comparison, Somers' (2009) results indicated that the organizational reliance potential survey (ORPS) is an acceptable tool to measure organization's reliance potential. Therefore, this revealed a difference in the type of result that the two studies produced. For example, Olofsson's results produced data to add to the theory of the OCPH model, whereas Somers' results indicated that a specific survey was acceptable to measure a specific theory. This measurement tool will help other researchers further develop the body of knowledge in future studies of organizational resilience, differing from Oloffson where no new measurement tool was developed.

In comparison of the two aforementioned studies, the results of the study by Coldwell et al. (2012) differed due the inclusion of qualitative and quantitative results. The qualitative case study analysis indicated that the speed of implementation of the responsibility compass has an effect on "individual company share prices" (Coldwell et. al., 2012, p. 142). The quantitative measurement, focusing on corporate reputation and brand strength, indicated a slight relationship between the selected company's reputation capital and the effects reputation capital has on resolution of share prices following a crisis. Therefore, when reliance is compared to brand strength, a similarity is presented because when a brand is strong, it can be viewed as reliable, which also has effects on reputation capital.

As indicated above, organizational crisis is often unexpected and may endanger organizational goals (Weick, 1988). The structure of an organization can significantly affect the level of organizational crisis when appropriate management is implemented to reduce negative impacts to the organization. Furthermore, individual organizational culture plays an important role in organizational change during organizational crisis (Rizescu, 2011). This became apparent in the CFD following June 18, 2007.

In strong support of this, Kroeber and Kluckhohn's (1952) research was utilized in the methodology of various studies. The researchers undertook an extensive analysis of the meaning of organizational culture with the study of more than 300 existing studies. This methodology indicated that diverse interpretations tested difficulties in synthetic circumscription with necessary and sufficient congruent features. It consisted of the efficiency of attitude and behavior, acquiring and transmitting symbols that celebrate achievements, as well as the utilization of default models (Rizescu, 2011). Further strengthening Rizescu's research, Schein (1992) stated that organizational culture involves climate, values, rituals, and behaviors that create a whole and are at the core of a culture (Rizescu, 2011). Dutch Professor Geert Hofstede claimed that organizational culture is difficult to change because of human activities involved (Rizescu, 2011). With the human complexes presented in organizations, the culture of an organization will be difficult to change, influencing the organizational changes necessary during an organizational crisis.

If not handled in a timely fashion, organizational crisis can intensify, resulting in damage to the organization's reputation and tearing down the organization to its core, with some instances being so severe that the organization cannot survive (Caywood & Stocker, 1993; Simola, 2005). The aforementioned study is relevant to this specific study as it indicated that when an organizational crisis becomes apparent, for example June 18, 2007, if it is not handled properly it will intensify, causing further damage to an already fragile organization. This is similar to the CFD's experience with an organizational crisis post June 18, 2007, where the organization and its leaders became fragile under the scrutiny of the media and reports pertaining to the event.

Simola (2005) indicated that some organizational crises are so severe that the organization cannot survive. In the case of a public service organization such as the CFD, the organization must survive because it is an organization that cannot cease to function. The organization is tasked with providing emergency services protection for over one hundred thousand citizens. Therefore, if the organization suffers such a severe crisis and cannot survive, the government will not be ensuring the safety of the citizens.

Organizational crisis places a tremendous amount of stress not only on the individuals employed by the organization, but also on the stakeholders due to the threats to the organizations goals and viability (Fink, 1986). Stakeholders play an intricate role in development and have the means to alter organizations (Hsu & Hannan, 2005). They examine organizations and determine whether to award resources to qualifying organizations (Tieyang et al., 2008). When organizational crisis strikes, stakeholders examine the valuation of the organization through its identity and may reduce the needed resources (Carroll & Hannan, 2000).

An organization's valuation is related to its organizational identity, which is referred to as social codes that identify the characteristics an organization ultimately possesses (Tieyang et al., 2008; Carroll & Hannan, 2000). This code-like status is made up of rules that have obvious consequences if violated (Carroll & Hannan, 2000). Tieyang et al. (2008) stated that "an organizational crisis is one such situation where stakeholders believe that the default social codes of the stricken organization are violated" (p. 454). Organizational crisis stimulates the learning process, where stakeholders of the effected organization evaluate the crisis and research the best course of organizational action to be taken (Weick, 1995). Organizational crisis can cause an effected organization to deviate from previous strategies and tactics, increasing the uncertainty of its future and effecting its survival (Tieyang et al., 2008). This became apparent in the CFD following June 18, 2007.

The research of Tieyang et al. (2008) indicated that the spread of negative aspects from an organizational crisis depends on the industry. Furthermore, they argued that correlating the characteristics of industries to the actions of organizations with frequent organizational crises, such as industries that rely on high risk-technologies, can enable an organization to create a more advantageous structure unaffected by crises or the negative impacts of crises (Tieyang et al., 2008). The fire service industry can be viewed as one of these types of industries with research indicating that 83 firefighters were killed in the line of duty in 2012, which proves that the fire service industry is affected by crises yearly (US Fire Administration, 2013).

One of these serious events occurred on June 18, 2007. The problems that surfaced in the CFD post June 18, 2007 were broadcasted in the media, as well as in studies focusing on the fire. When these negative impacts of the event spilled over to other departments, the errors made by the CFD were used to ensure that a tragedy such as this did not happen again. The fire service is an industry that relies on high-risk technologies and, therefore, if fire service industry characteristics can be linked together, then the industry can grow into a more robust industry where it is proactive rather than reactive.

The next theme is organizational learning, with a subtheme focused upon employee learning and development. Specific research is presented to identify how through organizational learning, an organization can recover from the grave consequences of organizational crisis. Also, a brief background and history of organizational learning is presented.

ORGANIZATIONAL LEARNING

Organizational learning is defined as a "regulated collective learning process in which individual and group-based learning experiences concerning the improvement of organizational performance and/or goals are transferred into organizational routines, processes and structures, which in turn effect the future learning activities of the organizations members" (Schilling & Kluge, 2009, p. 338).

This theory was first introduced by March et al. (1963) and Cangelosi and Dill (1965), and was viewed by scholars as one of the most effective theories of leadership (Schilling & Kluge, 2009; Toulabi et al., 2013). Since its introduction in the mid 1960s, it has received much attention from scholars, especially in the last 3 decades (Schilling & Kluge, 2009). The ability for organizations to learn creates a major source of competitive advantage for the future of organizations. More importantly, however, the ability of an organization to learn is a prerequisite for the survival of an organization (Lahteenmaki et al., 2001).

The organizational learning theory is divided into two distinct areas: single loop learning and double loop learning (Argyris, 2002). Single loop learning is defined as correcting errors without changing underlying governing values (Argyris, 2002). Comparatively, double loop learning is defined as correcting errors by altering the governing values and actions (Argyris, 2002). For example, a thermostat can be viewed as single loop learning because it is programmed to recognize when the temperature is too hot or too cold and turns the air on to adjust the temperature accordingly. If a thermostat was to change to double loop learning, it would have to question why it is programmed to monitor temperature and adjust the temperature to what it thinks is correct (Argyris, 2002).

Watkins and Marsick's (1997) model is rooted in the theory that "organizations are organic entities like individuals and have the capacity to learn" (Yang et al., 2004). This framework has distinctive characteristics, including a clear and concise definition of a learning organization that includes dimensions of learning at all levels in the organization. Redding (1997) posited following numerous reviews of other assessment tools for learning that Watkins and Marsick's DLOQ (1997) was one of the few that incorporated learning at all levels, including the individual, team, and organizational levels. Another advantage of this model is that it identifies the main dimensions of learning and also specifies their relationships. This in-depth model describes the seven dimensions of learning with the use of action imperatives, which offers the model more practical implications. This type of perspective provides a cultural perspective on the theory and identifies many actions that can be utilized to increase learning (Yang et al., 2004).

EMPLOYEE LEARNING AND DEVELOPMENT

COMMUNITY ORGANIZATIONAL LEARNING: CASE STUDIES ILLUSTRATING A THREE-DIMENSIONAL MODEL OF LEVELS AND ORDERS OF CHANGE

Organizational learning can produce superficial or fundamental differences in thinking and acting in organizations, including nonprofit, for-profit, and public service organizations. Regarding nonprofit organizations, a number of fire service organizations can be viewed this way. It is imperative that these types of organizations learn from previous experiences to continue the growth and success of said organization. To ascertain this information, the study's researchers asked three specific questions: "How do nonprofit organizations serve as contexts for individual learning and development?", "What are the key organizational learning characteristics of successful community-based nonprofits?", and "How do nonprofit organizations become effective agents of community change?" (Perkins et al., 2007, p. 309).

A two-year period was used to complete the three-phase study in a Southern mid-size city (Perkins et al., 2007). Phase one selected the sample from a compilation of databases from multiple sources. The sample consisted of 2,361 community nonprofit organizations. Phase two consisted of interviews via telephone with 270 organizations, with phase three's focus on the selection of 16 organizations. To advance the results, 39 individuals from the 16 organizations were interviewed using a semistructured format with open-ended questions about organizational goals, organizational crisis, efforts to inform local businesses or government about important issues, and new activities. The interviews were recorded, transcribed, and placed into NVivo, a coding software program for qualitative data (Perkins et al., 2007).

Results indicated second order change to be "progressively more challenging" at the individual or group levels as compared to community and organizational levels (Perkins et al., 2007, p. 322). On the individual level, organizations offer opportunities for task relation, role learning, and personal transformative change. Organizational change and sustainability are interdependent. To gain sustainability, organizations need to facilitate transformative learning and subsequent change. Furthermore, organizations and their employees need to continually learn to adapt to their changing environments (Perkins et al., 2007).

Perkins et al. (2007) presented strengths in that it studied organizational learning through a lens of empowerment, which has been a major concern in the psychology community; however, it has received less attention in the management literature. The alignment of the methodology was excellent as was the design, with the researchers completing a three-phase project consisting of the selection of the sample, participant interviews, and the selection of organizations to be utilized. Furthermore, the sample utilized was strong, with the incorporation of over 2,000 nonprofits, which allowed for more accurate research data to be obtained.

THE EFFECTS OF ORGANIZATIONAL LEARNING CULTURE AND JOB SATISFACTION ON MOTIVATION TO TRANSFER LEARNING AND TURNOVER INTENTION

Employee learning and development is essential for competitive success in the ever-changing world of innovation and technology. Major influences of this in an organization include culture, the amount of learning related events, employee satisfaction, and the motivation of employees to disseminate the information they have learned. Furthermore, scholars believe motivation to transfer learning is essential for the success of "organizational learning, performance, and investment" (Egan et al., 2004, p. 280). Is employee job satisfaction impacted by organizational learning culture? Are employee's motivations to transfer learning impacted by job satisfaction and organizational learning culture? How are employee's turnover intentions affected by job satisfaction and organizational learning culture (Egan et al., 2004)?

Three thousand three hundred and thirty six firms in the U.S. were selected and sent letters asking for their participation in the study (Egan et al., 2004). Fifty organizations agreed to participate, with a final number of 13 firms participating, completing 245 surveys total. The relationships between organizational learning culture, motivation to transfer learning, job satisfaction, and intention to turnover were investigated using a survey research method. Individual level perception information was collected from employees utilizing a self-administered, web-based survey (Egan et al., 2004).

Organizational learning culture was measured with The Dimensions of the Learning Organization Questionnaire (DLOQ) (Watkins

& Marsick, 1997). Next, The Michigan Organizational Assessment Questionnaire was used to measure job satisfaction. Finally, 10 items were utilized to measure the motivation to transfer items, with Irving, Coleman, and Cooper (1997) measuring turnover intention (Egan et al., 2004). Results indicated that organizational learning culture has significant positive contributions to motivation to transfer learning and job satisfaction. Furthermore, learning culture has a substantial impact on job satisfaction, significantly effecting turnover intention. Finally, learning culture is valid in predicting turnover intention in employees and is mediated by job satisfaction (Egan et al., 2004).

EFFECTS OF ORGANIZATIONAL LEARNING AND INFORMATION-PROCESSING BEHAVIORS ON NEW PRODUCT SUCCESS

Organizational learning, or the improvement of organizational decisions from experiences of past actions, is important to the success of new products. Can a model of organizational learning derived from information-processed constructs be formulated? If this model is found, does it affect the new product success rate? A judgmental sample of 38 firms that create high technology industrial products, including electronic components, instruments, computer products, advanced composite materials, and telecommunication equipment was used (Lynn et al., 1997). Questionnaires were utilized to gather the data about new product information retrieving, reviewing, and recording practices, with financial performance, new product performance, and research and development expenditure statistics as well. The chief research and development officer and the chief marketing officer from each firm completed the questionnaires by consensus. The items included in the measurement were developed from the literature and confirmed in interviews with the firms participating in the study. Results indicated that organizational learning has a positive impact on new product success. Furthermore, new product success is affected by the improvement of researching and tracking previous designs of products and the reaction the market sustained from these designs. This further proves the idea that records have to be created completely and retrieved easily due to the role they play in effective learning (Lynn et al., 1997).

SYNTHESIS OF THE LITERATURE

Organizational learning influences employee learning and development, along with the success of the product the employees are representing. Whether it is a product that is sold, a service, a nonprofit, for-profit, or public service organization, employee learning and development is essential to the continued success of an organization. Fundamental differences in thinking and acting in organizations are related to organizational culture, employee satisfaction, and the number of learning related events (Perkins et al., 2007; Egan et al., 2004). Different types of organizations will have different cultures; therefore, the way they think and act will be different as well. If organizations can learn from not only their past experiences, but past experiences from other organizations, either similar in profession or not, all organizations can increase their amount of organizational learning. This will improve future organizational decisions, which creates better products and services.

Studies focusing on organizational learning had relationships in their research questions. Individual learning and development are related to organizational learning culture and the impact it has on employee job satisfaction (Egan et al., 2004; Perkins et al., 2007). This relationship is present because employees will be satisfied with their profession if they are enabled to learn and develop into employees consistent with the organizational culture. Also similar is the question of the influence organizational learning culture has on job satisfaction on employee's motivation to pass on what they have learned with new product success rate (Egan et al., 2004; Lynn et al., 1997). Again, if employees are satisfied with their profession and the organizational culture they are a part of, the organization will be experiencing success. Furthermore, they are more likely to transfer information to other employees, which will ensure new product success because the formula that has worked for them to cause the success has now been transferred to new employees to ensure that success is continued.

The samples from the organizational learning literature were different with nonprofit organizations, U.S firms, and high technology firms utilized. Two of the study's samples were selected from thousands of participating organizations that were then scaled down to a smaller, more manageable sample of 16 organizations and 13 firms respectively, which is consistent with the 38 firms utilized in Egan's study (Egan et al., 2004; Lynn et al., 1997; Perkins et al., 2007).

Organizational learning has been studied using both quantitative and qualitative methods. The quantitative methods utilized differed in the studies with a self-administered, web-based survey and questionnaires utilized, respectively. Examples of these quantitative approaches consisted of the study of Ellinger et al. (2002), where they assessed the relationship between the learning organization concept and the firms' financial performance empirically. There is also Sahaya (2012), who studied a learning organization as a mediator of leadership style and a firms' financial performance. Qualitative methods utilized interviews that were recorded, transcribed, and put into NVivo, a coding program for qualitative data, whereas the web-based survey measured individual level perception with The Dimensions of the Learning Organization Questionnaire (Egan et al., 2004; Perkins et al., 2007). Examples of qualitative studies focusing on organizational learning included Gau and Wen's (2011) study and Yeung, Lai, and Yee's (2007) study.

In further comparison, the findings of Egan et al. (2004), which indicated that organizational learning culture has significant positive contributions on motivation to transfer learning and job satisfaction, was related to the findings of Lynn et al. (1997), which indicated that organizational learning has a positive impact on new product success (Egan et al., 2004; Lynn et al., 1997). This relationship was apparent because the positive effects of employees' satisfaction with their jobs will create opportunities for them to transfer knowledge to other employees, which will in turn ensure the success of new products. When a successful organization learns from its success and continues to promote this success and level of development in its employees, this will translate into the quality of the products or services they develop or offer. Another similarity in the literature is the fact that organizations need to continually learn about and adapt to their environment (Perkins et al., 2007).

This can be done by creating records that are not only forthcoming, but also concise and easily retrieved so the organization can learn from the past and adapt more adequately (Lynn et al., 1997).

The current study aimed to identify how the CFD learned following an organizational crisis at the individual, team, and organizational levels focusing on the above mentioned collective learning process that consisted of single and double loop learning. This was made possible with the use of triangulation that incorporated Watkins and Marsick's DLOQ (1997). Furthermore, with the inclusion of interviews and artifact analysis, all levels of learning were able to be identified to offer sound scientific research to other organizations that may suffer the grave consequences of organizational crisis.

SUMMARY

Organizational crisis is a dynamic of an organization that puts extreme amounts of stress on an organization's leaders, employees, employee families, the citizens the organization serves, and its stakeholders (James, 2007). High-reliability organizations such as the fire service, law enforcement, military, and medical responders are presented with the challenge of responding to unsafe, unstable, and consistently changing situations and environments that can grow into an organizational crisis. Comparatively, organizational learning, which is divided into single and double loop learning, is an organizationally "regulated collective learning process in which individual and group-based learning experiences concerning the improvement of organizational performance and/or goals are transferred into organizational routines, processes and structures, which in turn affect the future learning activities of the organizations members" (Schilling & Kluge, 2009, p. 338). Since its introduction in the mid 1960's by March et al. (1963) and Cangelosi and Dill (1965), it has received much attention from scholars, especially in the last three decades (Schilling & Kluge, 2009).

The current study extended research conducted by James (2007) that focused on organizational learning after the organizational crisis that ensued following NASA's Columbia tragedy. James' findings indicated that NASA learned from their previous lack of transparency following the Challenger disaster and enhanced their organization as a result. This enhancement gave them the knowledge to combat a future organizational crisis following the Columbia disaster.

This study addressed the omission in the existing literature by researching how an organization like the CFD learned from an organizational crisis following the multiple LODD's that occurred on June 18, 2007 in The City of Charleston Fire Department. The incident studied presented challenges for the leaders of the fire department, a high reliability organization, to respond to the unsafe, unstable, and consistently changing events that occurred (Baran & Scott, 2010). Since the majority of leadership research focused on learning in stable conditions, this incident was used to research how an organization like the CFD learned from a crisis that presented unstable, unsafe, and constantly changing conditions to fill the apparent gap in the literature (Baran & Scott, 2010). Furthermore, the individual, team, and organizational levels were focused upon as they are essential components of organizational learning and development whether during times of organizational crisis or times of success.

Chapter 2 provided an extensive review of the literature of the studied constructs. Chapter 3 focuses on the methodology of the study and includes research methodology, research design, data collection procedures, data analysis procedures, limitations, population and sample information, sources of data, validity, reliability, and ethical considerations. These sections allow the reader to have an in-depth look at the specifics of how the data was collected, analyzed, and how the participants were treated throughout the study.

CHAPTER 3
Methodology

INTRODUCTION

Shuhui Sophy and Seeger (2012) noted how organizational crises present important organizational learning lessons. Furthermore, Weick (1988) stated that organizational crisis is unexpected and endangers organizational goals. When high reliability organizations such as the fire service experience unexpected crises, it is difficult for responders to make sense of the unstable, unsafe, and rapidly changing environments that they respond to (Baran & Scott, 2010). When an organization is faced with a crisis, the dynamics of the organizational changes place extreme amounts of stress on organizational leaders, employees, and stakeholders (James, 2007).

The purpose of this case study was to identify how an organization like the CFD learned from an organizational crisis following June 18, 2007 at the individual, team, and organizational levels. Unfortunately, fire service organizations all over the world experience LODD's yearly. The identification of how an organization like the CFD learned from an organizational crisis at the individual, team, and organizational levels is essential to gain a better understanding of the problem in order to indicate how a crisis changed organizational processes and employee behaviors.

This chapter includes in-depth explanations of the research methodology employed throughout the study. Specifically, it includes descriptions of the research design, the sources of data, and the chosen sample, with an explanation of why they were selected. Also included are sections discussing the validity and reliability of the instruments used. Finally, data collection procedures, ethical considerations, and the limitations of the study are presented.

STATEMENT OF THE PROBLEM

It was not known how an organization like the CFD learned from an organizational crisis at the individual, team, and organizational levels. Specifically, this study investigated how the CFD as an organization learned from the crisis of the June 18, 2007 incident through organizational learning.

RESEARCH QUESTION(S)

The overarching question of this study was: How were organizational processes and employee behaviors changed following a crisis? This overarching question was answered by the guidance of the research questions, which included the following:

R1: How did the CFD learn from organizational crisis at the individual level?

R2: How did the CFD learn from organizational crisis at the team level?

R3: How did the CFD learn from organizational crisis at the organizational level?

These research questions directed the focus of the study with triangulation utilizing the DLOQ (Watkins & Marsick, 1997), one-on-one interviews, and artifact analysis. First, the DLOQ (Watkins & Marsick, 1997) is a questionnaire that all participants completed with specific instructions to provide evidence for the three research questions. Included in the instructions to the participants, the phrase, "Do you believe since June 18, 2007 . . ." was added as a preface for each question in the DLOQ. Therefore, the question read as follows: Do you believe since June 18, 2007, "In my organization, people openly discuss mistakes in order to learn from them?" (Marsick & Watkins, 2003, p. 143).

Five of these participants were randomly selected to participate in an interview with the researcher and were asked the following questions created by an expert panel of command level officers in the fire service, where each had over 30 years' of fire service experience. These questions were developed focusing on the individual, team, and organizational levels of the CFD. The first interview question asked the participants how the CFD discusses mistakes to allow its members and the fire service to learn from them. This question adds evidence to support R1. The second question regarding how the CFD utilized committees to support the direction of the department adds evidence to support R2. The third question, how does the CFD ensure that all employees are aware of lessons learned from previous emergency and training incidents, contributes supportive evidence to R3. Secondarily, a fourth question that asks, how have you learned and improved as a firefighter since June 18, 2007, adds more depth to R1. Finally, the question of how the CFD's leadership has changed since June 18, 2007 adds greater depth to R3.

The third source of research utilized in the triangulation of data sources was the use of artifact analysis, which highlighted the CFD since June 18, 2007. These artifacts consisted of newspaper articles, the CFD's Strategic Plan, CFD standard operating procedures, CFD memos, CFD policies, and other fire service articles pertaining to the CFD following June 18, 2007. These artifacts indicated specific areas where the CFD made significant operational, training, and leadership changes. Furthermore, the research presented from these artifacts focused upon the individual, team, and organizational levels to ensure successful correlation between all three sources utilized in the triangulation.

Webb et al. (1966) proposed the idea of the unobtrusive method, which is one of the earliest references to triangulation. He stated that "once a proposition has been confirmed by two or more independent measurement processes, the uncertainty of its interpretation is greatly reduced. The most persuasive evidence comes through a triangulation of measurement processes" (p. 3). In this study, the role of each data source in the triangulation will add to the certainty that the data collected is consistent with the researcher's claims. Furthermore, such a rigorous design enhanced the quality of the findings of this research as perceptions from responders were correlated with internal and external artifact data to add to the responder's indications and decrease the chances of bias due to utilizing only internal sources or one source of data collection.

Gathering perceptions from responders of June 18, 2007 of how an organization like the CFD learned from organizational crisis at the individual, team, and organizational levels provides other organizations with scientific research of how they can learn from their own respective organizational crisis in the event that one was to occur. Furthermore, providing evidence of how an organization like the CFD learned from an organizational crisis in this manner offers scientific evidence of examples successfully used by other organizations.

RESEARCH METHODOLOGY

This is a qualitative case study seeking data from firefighters from the CFD using triangulation, incorporating data collected through the DLOQ instrument (Watkins & Marsick, 1997), interviews, and artifact analysis. Specifically, sampled participants completed Watkins and Marsick's (1997) Dimensions of the Learning Organization Questionnaire (DLOQ) and five were randomly selected for an interview with the researcher utilizing open-ended questions that were developed by command level officers in the fire service, each with 30 years' of fire service experience. The final source in the triangulation was the use of artifact data analysis, including the CFD's Strategic Plan, CFD standard operating procedures, CFD memos, CFD policies, newspaper articles, and other fire service articles pertaining to the CFD following June 18, 2007.

A case study was chosen as they can provide in-depth perspectives that lead to a rich understanding of problems, can focus on natural or social events, such as a response to a disaster, and can have the subject be an organization, an individual, or any other entity (Marrelli, 2007). They offer a multi-perspectival analysis, meaning that the researchers take into account not only the actor's voice and perspectives, but also the interaction between the actors and relevant groups (Feagin et al. 1991). However, they also have their weaknesses. Shen (2009) stated that studying a small case number might not offer any support for generality or reliability of research findings. Additionally, Nisbet and Watt (1984) suggested that the results of case studies do not often employ crosschecking, meaning that they may be biased, subjective, personal, and selective, despite efforts to identify reflexivity.

A qualitative method was utilized as this method enables the study of phenomena of human beings in their natural setting. The main advantage of qualitative research is that it allows phenomena to be grasped from participant views (Toloie-Eshlaghy et al., 2011). This is always neglected when using a quantitative method rather than a qualitative one (Toloie-Eshlaghy et al., 2011). Additionally, potential data sources in a qualitative method may incorporate archival records, documentation, physical artifacts, interviews, and participant observation (Baxter & Jack, 2008). Additionally, the qualitative design for this study centered on a case study. The research indicated that a case study is "unique in comparison to other qualitative approaches" allowing investigators to "collect and integrate quantitative survey data, which facilitates reaching a holistic understanding of the phenomenon being studied" (Baxter & Jack, 2008, p. 554). This directly related to the current study due to the utilization of Watkins and Marsick's (1997) DLOQ as a part of the data collection process.

However, weaknesses are present in qualitative data collection. Duffy (1985) posited that the methodology is described as phenomenology, or according to Leach (1990), an idealistic or humanistic approach where the origin is derived from psychology, anthropology, history, philosophy, and sociology (Cormack, 1991). According to Carr (1994), scholars view this as one of qualitative research's greatest weaknesses, as this foundation does not present physical science characteristics.

For the purpose of this study the qualitative method was selected, as the researcher aimed to gather perceptions from the sampled participants and to attain data from three different sources, rather than quantifying data from one source. Furthermore, the researcher aimed to study phenomena of the participants in their natural setting, as this provided evidence of learning in the CFD at the individual, team, and organizational levels. This method provided richer, more in-depth research regarding the CFD following June 18, 2007, as selected participants were able to speak at length regarding the CFD while providing answers to open-ended questions supported with the responses from the DLOQ (Watkins & Marsick, 1997) and artifact data.

When deciding on either the experimental or non-experimental approach, the choice is steered primarily by the research questions (Price, 2012). It is impossible to replicate the crisis that occurred in 2007, and it is also impossible to obtain objective, un-biased pre-crisis data at this time (6 years later). Therefore, the study only focused on current data, in further support of a non-experimental approach, to most effectively and efficiently address the research questions posed in the study. Additionally, Price (2012) suggested that non-experimental research presents strengths when the research questions are exploratory and broad, or when attempting to study a specific experience. It is weak, however, because it does not address third variable problems and directionality with the use of control and manipulation of variables through the use of random assignments (Price, 2012). Further, this study did not seek to discern why organizational learning occurred in the CFD, eliminating the value of using an experimental design approach. The weaknesses of a non-experimental design are not of relevance to this study.

This case study design accomplished the study's goals because it allowed for multiple sources of data to be utilized to answer the research questions, rather than employing the use of a single source. It was the optimal choice for the current study, as research indicated that qualitative case studies with a non-experimental approach provide for a multi-perspectival analysis that focuses on the study of phenomena of human beings in their natural setting or the study of a specific experience. The current study utilized this method, and with the multi-perspectival analysis of firefighters in their natural setting following the experience of the June 18, 2007 incident, this method was a good fit.

RESEARCH DESIGN

A qualitative case study utilizing triangulation was used to collect the data for this investigation. This design was chosen because it most effectively addressed the research questions, as three sources of data collection allowed for the production of richer, more in-depth qualitative research and allowed for the study of phenomenon in its natural setting, rather than the testing of theories with the examination of variables. The researcher utilized triangulation to gather specific data regarding the CFD and its members. Included in the triangulation was Watkins and Marsick's DLOQ (1997), interviews utilizing five open-ended questions developed by a panel of three command level officers in the fire service, each with over 30 years' of experience, and artifact analysis.

Toloie-Eshlaghy et al. (2011) stated that an advantage of qualitative research methods is that it allows for the study of phenomena of human beings in their natural setting. More specifically, this type of research encourages phenomena to be grasped from participant views, which is always neglected when utilizing a quantitative approach (Toloie-Eshlaghy et al., 2011). Additionally, Baxter and Jack (2008) posited that potential data sources in a qualitative method may incorporate archival records, documentation, physical artifacts, interviews, and participant observation. "Unique in comparison to other qualitative approaches, within case study research, investigators can collect and integrate quantitative survey data, which facilitates reaching a holistic understanding of the phenomenon being studied" (p. 554). This directly relates to the current study due to the utilization of Watkins and Marsick's (1997) DLOQ as a part of the data collection process.

Case studies have unique characteristics that were more beneficial to this type of study rather than other qualitative designs such as ethnography, grounded theory, or phenomenology. Specifically, Stake (2003) suggested that a "case study is defined by interest in individual cases, not by the methods of inquiry used," where the primary criteria for selection is the "opportunity to learn" (p. 134; Stake, 1995, p. 6). Marrelli (2007) added to this research, stating that case studies provide in-depth perspectives that can lead to a rich understanding of problems, can focus on natural or social events such as a response to a disaster, and the subject can either be an organization, an individual, or any other entity. Case studies are a multi-perspectival analysis, meaning that the researchers take into account not only the actor's voice and perspectives, but also the interaction between the actors and relevant groups (Feagin et al., 1991). This is an important point in case studies characteristics. A voice is given to the "powerless and voiceless" (Tellis, 1997, p. 1). When studies are presented by sociological investigations on the homeless and powerless, they are done from the "elite" viewpoint (Feagin et al., 1991; Tellis, 1997).

Questionnaires have many advantages that make them a good choice for data collection (Jones et al., 2008). They are low cost and there is a minimal amount of training that must be given to the individuals administering them and the individuals taking them (Jones et al., 2008). Questionnaires enable a researcher to reach larger participant numbers in a population than is possible with interviews, and they can be delivered electronically, via the web, or by telephone (Jones et al., 2008). Furthermore, the data from the DLOQ (Watkins & Marsick, 1997) specifically can help identify where the changes exist at the individual, team, and organizational levels.

Palmerino (1999) posited that interviews offer increased value of research and should be considered by researchers more often. Additionally, Jacob and Furgerson (2012) stated that the primary way in which researchers collect individual's stories and study specific aspects of the human experience is through interviews. They highlight each and every respondent's best thinking and every word spoken by the respondent can be utilized in multiple ways (Palmerino, 1999). The interview data added depth needed to explain the changes identified by the DLOQ (Watkins & Marsick, 1997).

Data collected from this qualitative case study included the utilization of a triangulation incorporating Watkins and Marsick's DLOQ (1997), interviews, and artifact analysis. The researcher first electronically mailed the responders a recruitment letter to explain the study (Appendix C, on page XXV). A consent form was also included upon their agreement to participate (Appendix D, on page XXVI). This form stated that the study was confidential and that they were not required to include any personal information. Also, the consent form included language that stated the participants could withdraw from the study at any time.

All participants were electronically mailed a link to Kwiksurveys.com in order to access the DLOQ (Watkins & Marsick, 1997). The participants accessed the link and completed the questionnaire with specific instructions. These instructions included the addition of the phrase "Do you believe since June 18, 2007" preceding every question. For example, the following is a question from the DLOQ that measures the individual level: "In my organization, people openly discuss mistakes in order to learn from them" (Marsick & Watkins, 2003, p. 143). With the addition of the specific instructions, the question read as follows: Do you believe since June 18, 2007, "In my organization, people openly discuss mistakes in order to learn from them?" (Marsick & Watkins, 2003, p. 143). Possible ratings for the above question, as well as for the other measurement questions, were 1-6, where 1 was almost never and 6 was almost always.

The researcher then interviewed five of these participants with the following questions created by an expert panel of three command level officers, each with over 30 years' of fire experience. The first question asked the participants, how does the CFD discuss mistakes to allow its members and the fire service to learn from them. Second, how does the CFD utilize committees to support the direction of the department? Third, how does the CFD ensure that all employees are aware of lessons learned from previous emergency and training incidents? Fourth, how have you learned and improved as a firefighter since June 18, 2007? Finally, how has the CFD's leadership changed since June 18, 2007?

The third source of data utilized in the triangulation was the use of artifacts that highlighted the CFD since June 18, 2007. These artifacts consisted of newspaper articles, the CFD's Strategic Plan, CFD standard operating procedures, CFD memos, CFD policies, and fire service articles relating to the CFD following June 18, 2007. These data sources indicated specific areas where the CFD made significant operational, training, and leadership changes.

Ascertaining how the CFD learned from an organizational crisis in this manner provides other organizations with scientific research of how they can learn from their own respective organizational crisis if they were to experience one. Also, identifying how the CFD learned from an organizational crisis at these three levels offers organizations information to help them recognize that they may be currently experiencing or on the road to experiencing an organizational crisis. As stated by Brong (2004), relative to NASA's organizational crisis, it is an extraordinary responsibility for the organization to learn from the incident, therefore, it is also an extraordinary responsibility for the CFD to do the same. The qualitative case study design was the best approach for this study, as the substantial and specific grounds of participants produced data that added to the body of knowledge of organizational crisis and organizational learning.

Furthermore, this study influences practices in the field as organizations will now have research indicating how an organization like the CFD learned from an organizational crisis following a multiple LODD at the individual, team, and organizational levels. This much needed literature expansion will aid not only public service organizations in better decision-making, but in many other types of organizations as well. Additionally, the opportunity to learn from human beings that responded to the incident in their natural setting with questionnaires, interviews, and artifact analysis indicated how the CFD learned at the individual, team, and organizational levels from the incident on June 18, 2007.

POPULATION AND SAMPLE SELECTION

The population for the current study included firefighters that could face crisis and benefit from organizational learning. More specifically, the setting for the study was The City of Charleston Fire Department in Charleston, South Carolina, where the current workforce at the time of the study was 318 firefighters who protected 120,000 citizens according to the 2010 census. Since June 18, 2007, the CFD hired over 240 new employees and has since lost approximately 25% of these employees, as well as 25% of the incumbents that were employed with the CFD prior to June 18, 2007 (Firehouse Reporting, 2013). Therefore, the current 318 employees were affected by the crisis, whether they were with the organization before June 18, 2007 or not, as this crisis had led to continuous change since that tragic day in 2007.

In order to attain sample participants from the focused population, the researcher utilized purposive and convenience sampling. According to Gledhill, Abbey, and Schweitzer (2008), purposive sampling is utilized frequently for the obtainment of data in qualitative research and is often used when samples are studied with "focused methods such as in-depth interviews" (p. 85). Regarding convenience sampling, Kelley, Clark, Brown, and Sitzia (2008) stated that this type of sampling is a part of non-random sampling, which is applied commonly when qualitative methods are utilized to gather data. In a convenience sample, the participants are individuals within a population that were targeted deliberately and who were the easiest to recruit.

From the 21 sampled participants attained from purposive and convenience sampling, five were randomly selected to participate in the interview process included in the study. According to Kelley et al. (2008), random sampling allows study research to be generalized to a larger population. The utilization of this technique allows for each individual within the specified population to be chosen by chance and given the opportunity to be as equally selected as anyone else.

The three aforementioned sampling approaches connected to the method that the researcher utilized to attain the participants. Specifically, 27 firefighters that officially responded to the June 18, 2007 incident and were still employed with the CFD at the time of this study were contacted. Before June 18, 2007, the CFD was comprised of 246 members, with only 140 of these members remaining with the CFD in 2013. Therefore, out of the 318 current employees, 140 of them were from the time period before June 18, 2007, while all of the current 318 employees were affected by this crisis as the department continues to progress through the change process following the inci-dent. The remaining members were all male, ranging in ranks from firefighter to the chief officer level. Ages ranged from 25 to 60 years of age and experience in the fire service ranged from 1 to 40 years.

This data included the only information given regarding the characteristics of the remaining members of the CFD that responded to June 18, 2007 as the researcher does not want to give too much information that will allow for the identification of the study's par-ticipants. All individuals within the population were invited to par-ticipate, although some were reluctant to do so. The final purposive and convenience sample numbered 21 participants.

This sample included a large number of the responders, which added to the production of rich and in-depth data. Race, gender, and rank structure were not discussed, as this information would draw attention to the study's participants. The Firehouse software includ-ing the responder list can be accessed by firefighters. In addition, if the researcher provided specificity of rank and race, the responder list could be correlated with the participants, negating the anony-mous study.

The 27 possible participants were the official responders to June 18, 2007, as recorded on the incident report in the Firehouse reporting software, and were obtained by the researcher electronic mailing them a recruitment letter (Appendix C, on page XXV) and consent form (Appendix D, on page XXVI). A meeting was not held with all of the participants as the researcher wanted to keep all of them separate throughout the process in order to decrease bias. If they agreed, they electronically mailed the researcher back expressing their interest.

The participants were then electronically mailed a link to complete the DLOQ (Watkins & Marsick, 1997), as well as electronically mailed information if they were randomly selected as one of the five interview participants. Confidentiality measures included numerical designations given to interview participants and the utilization of Kwiksurveys.com to attain the questionnaire data. The participants were electronically mailed a link to complete the questionnaire, where the results were stored on Kwiksurveys.com with no personal information included.

Five participants for the interviews were then randomly selected from those who completed the DLOQ (Watkins & Marsick, 1997). Specifically, the researcher transcribed all 21 participants' names on separate pieces of 2" x 2" pieces of paper, which were folded four times and placed in a 10" x 10" square box. The researcher then shook the box in a clockwise motion 10 times and placed the box on a desk. The researcher blindfolded himself, opened the box, and selected five of the 2" x 2" pieces of paper that had the participants' names on them.

The artifact data was then chosen based on currency, as well as data that highlighted the CFD at the individual, team, and organizational levels. By ensuring that the artifact data focused on these three levels, it was possible to correlate all three sources in the triangulation. Furthermore, it added information to answer the important overarching question of this study: How were organizational processes and employee behaviors changed following a crisis?

All of the questionnaire, interview, and artifact analysis data were stored on the researcher's personal computer, with two back up devices stored in a locked safe inside the home of the researcher.

The safe has only two keys, the locations of which are known only by the researcher; the computer and back-up devices are all password protected. All of the data will be kept for seven years under these protected conditions.

SOURCES OF DATA

The research instruments used for this study were (1) The Dimensions of the Learning Organization Questionnaire (DLOQ) (Watkins & Marsick, 1997), which is a Likert-style self-assessment, (2) interviews utilizing five open-ended questions developed by three command level officers in the fire service, each with over 30 years' of fire service experience, respectively, and (3) artifact analysis. The DLOQ (Watkins & Marsick, 1997) consisted of the individual level, the team level, and the organizational level. The questions included: what is the role of the participant in the organization, what is their educational experience, how many employees are in their organization, what type of business is being studied, and what is the organization's annual revenue?

The questions from the DLOQ actually form seven dimensions consisting of continuous learning, inquiry and dialogue, team learning, embedded systems, empowerment, system connection, and strategic leadership (Watkins & Marsick, 1997). These seven dimensions were used to examine the individual, team, and organizational levels of an organization, where scoring ranged from a 1 to 6, with 1 being almost never and 6 almost always. Scores 2, 3, 4, and 5 indicated increasing ratings from almost never (1) to almost always (6). The mean scores were not compared to other organizations mean scores on the DLOQ and norms for the DLOQ were not applied to this research as no other study has been conducted in this manner following a multiple LODD (Watkins & Marsick, 1997). Questions 1-13 measured the individual level; questions 14-19 measured the team or group level; questions 20-43 measured the organizational level; questions 44-55 measured performance at the organizational level; and questions 56-62 measured additional information about the participant and the organization with multiple-choice answers for each respective question.

The aforementioned questions incorporated the seven key dimensions that guided the DLOQ (Watkins & Marsick, 1997). They were developed to identify, at the individual level, where opportunities for growth and education are provided, allowing for learning to occur on the job and creating an organizational culture that supports collective ideas where personnel listen and inquire to others about their views. At the team level, the key dimensions guided questions that focused on the encouragement of an environment conducive to collaboration, as well as systems in place to integrate this collaboration with work. At the organizational level, the questions were guided by the dimensions that stimulate the creation of a shared vision through empowerment and the link of the organization to the community along with leadership that utilizes strategic learning (Watkins & Marsick, 1997).

These seven dimensions were also considered by the expert panel of three command level officers in the development of the five open-ended questions utilized after the completion of the DLOQ (Watkins & Marsick, 1997) by five randomly selected participants. These open-ended questions included:

1. How does the CFD discuss mistakes to allow its members and the fire service to learn from them?
2. How does the CFD utilize committees to support the direction of the department?
3. How does the CFD ensure that all employees are aware of lessons learned from previous emergency and training incidents?
4. How have you learned and improved as a firefighter since June 18, 2007?
5. How has the CFD's leadership changed since June 18, 2007?

Questions one and four relate to the individual level of the DLOQ (Watkins & Marsick, 1997), as they focused on the discussion of mistakes to allow for the opportunity for others to learn, which were similar to the DLOQ's (Watkins & Marsick, 1997) continuous learning and inquiry and dialogue dimensions that addressed opportunities for growth and education, the encouragement of on the job learning, and the creation of a collective learning organizational culture. Question two related to the team level of the DLOQ (Watkins & Marsick, 1997), as it focused on the department's use of committees, which is similar to the team learning and embedded systems dimensions of the DLOQ (Watkins & Marsick, 1997) that encourage a collaborative culture where learning is shared. Questions three and five were related to the organizational level of the DLOQ (Watkins & Marsick, 1997) in that they attempted to ascertain how members were empowered to make all lessons learned available and how CFD leadership has impacted the organization at all levels since June 18, 2007. In comparison, the DLOQ's (Watkins & Marsick, 1997) empowerment, system connection, and strategic leadership dimensions outlined this level as they focused on accountability, the effect organizational members' work has on the organization, and how the CFD leaders set the example for the organization. The answers to these questions from the five randomly selected participants provided deeper insights into the data collected from the DLOQ (Watkins & Marsick, 1997).

Artifact data from newspaper articles, the CFD's Strategic Plan, CFD memos, CFD policies, CFD standard operating procedures, along with other fire service journal articles were then included in the data collection to add more support for the perceptions of the participants. All of the artifact data were organized at the individual, team, and organizational levels in preparation for final analysis. During this analysis, the two previous sources of data at each level were correlated with the artifacts. This added more depth to the study as the perceptions were supported by published internal and external documents regarding the CFD following June 18, 2007. By including both internal and external types of artifacts with the perceptions from a questionnaire and interviews, the researcher attempted to ensure the final data provided a view of the big picture of the CFD, rather than just the views of the participants.

VALIDITY

Numerous studies, including those of Yang et al. (1998), and Yang et al. (2004), have been completed to test the validity of the DLOQ (Watkins & Marsick, 1997). According to Davis and Daley (2008), the aforementioned authors presented evidence for this validity from "best model-data fit among alternative measurement models, nomological network among dimensions of the learning organization, and organizational performance outcomes" (p. 55). Confirmatory factor analysis (CFA) was used to measure construct validity for the DLOQ (Watkins & Marsick, 1997). Yang et al. (2004) indicated that this method was appropriate because it identified whether the suggested dimensions of a learning organization attributed characteristics that may provide "organized interpretations of learning behaviors" (p. 38). Structural equation modeling was then utilized to identify the relationships between organizational performance measures and the dimensions of the learning organization (Yang et al., 2004). Alternative models examined the construct validity of the model and this indicated a need to validate the instrument concisely, which "included only those items that most accurately represented the designated dimensions from statistical and substantive viewpoints" (Yang, 2004, p. 390).

The validity of the five open-ended interview questions developed by the expert panel of command level officers should be discussed as well. Young (2007) stated that in case research, it is not uncommon for the consultation of third party experts. Additionally, Seeger (2006) posited that expert panels from a specific field "may be asked to generate normative standards and principle's characteristic of effectiveness and efficiency" (p. 233). The current panel of three command level officers, each with over 30 years' of fire service experience, was considered to be comprised of third-party experts, all of who have generated normative standards and best practices in the national fire service due to their high level of experience and expertise. This made them sufficient experts on the topic, capable of producing valid open-ended questions. No information will be given regarding their rank, title, or department represented to ensure the total anonymity of the panel.

The artifact data analysis included in the triangulation was guided by the two sets of data above, making the analysis focused. The seven dimensions of the DLOQ (Watkins & Marsick, 1997), as well as the individual, team, and organizational levels laid the foundation of the perceptions. The answers to the open-ended questions were then added to increase the depth of the participant answers to the DLOQ (Watkins & Marsick, 1997), with the artifact data analysis completing the triangulation in a focused manner to ensure internal and external sources were utilized to support the participant's perceptions.

Refer to the tables below from Yang et al. (2004) for more information regarding the validity of the DLOQ (Watkins & Marsick, 1997) (Table 1, on page 113 and Table 2, on page 114). Permission was granted to utilize the tables for this study via electronic mail.

TABLE 1

Fit Indices for Alternative Measurement Models in the Simple and Complex Factor Structures of Learning Construct for Exploratory and Confirmatory Samples

Fit Index	Simple Factor Structure			Complex Structure
	Null Model	One-Factor	Seven-Factor	Seven-Factor
Exploratory Sample				
X2	11211.06	3630.98	2740.77	2031.88
df	861	819	798	778
X2 / df	13.02	4.43	3.43	2.61
RMSEA	0.17	0.09	0.08	0.06
RMSR	0.39	0.06	0.05	0.05
GFI	0.13	0.67	0.76	0.82
AGFI	0.09	0.64	0.73	0.79
NNFI (TLI)	0	0.71	0.80	0.87
CFI	0	0.73	0.81	0.88
Confirmatory Sample				
X2	12378.21	3517.09	2904.96	2746.29
df	861	819	798	778
x2 / df	14.38	4.29	3.64	3.53
RMSEA	0.18	0.09	0.08	0.08
RMSR	0.43	0.06	0.06	0.06
GFI	0.11	0.67	0.73	0.75
AGFI	0.07	0.64	0.69	0.71
NNFI (TLI)	0	0.75	0.80	0.81
CFI	0	0.77	0.82	0.83

Note: RMSEA = root mean square error of approximation; RMSR = root mean square residual; GFI = goodness-fit-index; AGI = adjusted GFI; NNFI = non-normed fit index; CFI = comparative fit index.

TABLE 2

Fit Indices for Alternative Measurement Models in the Simple and Complex Factor Structures of Performance Outcome for Exploratory and Confirmatory Samples

Fit Index	Simple Factor Structure			Complex Structure
	Null Model	One-Factor	Two-Factor	Two-Factor
Exploratory Sample				
X2	1696.33	452.46	413.40	208.62
Df	66	54	53	49
X2 / df	25.71	8.38	7.80	4.26
RMSEA	0.24	0.13	0.13	0.09
RMSR	0.32	0.08	0.08	0.05
GFI	0.44	0.84	0.86	0.93
AGFI	0.33	0.77	0.80	0.89
NNFI (TLI)	0	0.70	0.73	0.87
CFI	0	0.76	0.78	0.90
Confirmatory Sample				
X2	1949.40	333.70	317.65	284.53
Df	66	54	53	49
x2 / df	29.54	6.18	5.99	5.81
RMSEA	0.26	0.11	0.11	0.11
RMSR	0.36	0.06	0.06	0.06
GFI	0.37	0.89	0.89	0.91
AGFI	0.25	0.84	0.84	0.85
NNFI (TLI)	0	0.82	0.83	0.83
CFI	0	0.85	0.86	0.88

Note: RMSEA = root mean square error of approximation; RMSR = root mean square residual; GFI = goodness-fit-index; AGI = adjusted GFI; NNFI = non-normed fit index; CFI = comparative fit index.

RELIABILITY

Yang et al. (1998) and Yang et al. (2004) also conducted many tests to ensure the reliability of the DLOQ (Watkins & Marsick, 1997). Specifically, previous studies using the DLOQ found that it is reliable with a coefficient alpha ranging between .75 and .85. Watkins and Marsick (2003) focused on ensuring the reliability of the questionnaire as well. They stated that they put the tool through "rigorous critique for meaning," utilized "reliability coefficients to identify poorly worded items and low performing items," and continued to "delete or revise items until coefficient alphas for each scale were acceptable" (Watkins & Marsick, 2003, p. 136).

Therefore, Watkins and Marsick (1997) added new information to the DLOQ until the seven constructs of the tool exceeded .70 Cronbach's alpha coefficient (Watkins and Marsick, 2003). Davis (2005) found alpha coefficients ranging between .79 and .93. McHargue (1999) had alpha coefficients in the range from .75 to .85. In support of these ranges in reliability of the DLOQ (Watkins & Marsick, 1997), Wallen and Fraenkel (2001) expressed, "for research purposes, a rule of thumb is that reliability should be at least .70 and preferably higher" (p. 101). Refer to Table 3, on page 116 and Table 4, on page 117 from Yang et al. (2004) below for more information regarding the reliability of the DLOQ (Watkins & Marsick, 1997). Permission was granted to utilize the tables for this study via electronic mail.

TABLE 3

Means, Standard Deviations, Reliabilities and Zero-Order

Intercorrelations Among Dimensions of the Learning Organization

Variables[A]	N	M	SD	1	2	3	4	5	6	7	8	9
1. Continuous Learning	836	3.90	0.92	(.81)[b]								
2. Inquiry and Dialogue	836	3.79	0.92	0.75	(.87)							
3. Team Learning	833	3.85	0.96	0.71	0.74	(.86)						
4. Embedded Systems	834	3.34	0.99	0.63	0.58	0.64	(.81)					
5. Empowerment	833	3.66	0.97	0.66	0.67	0.71	0.67	(.84)				
6. System Connection	834	3.93	0.96	0.67	0.64	0.67	0.62	0.77	(.80)			
7. Provide Leadership	835	4.13	0.98	0.70	0.70	0.68	0.65	0.76	0.76	(.87)		
8. Financial Performance	819	4.13	0.95	0.37	0.35	0.42	0.33	0.36	0.37	0.41	(.74)	
9. Knowledge Performance	821	4.10	0.97	0.29	0.45	0.48	0.44	0.50	0.51	0.51	0.59	(.77)

Note: This was a two-tailed test; all of the correlation coefficients

are significant at the level of $p < .001$.

[A]Each dimension measured by a six-point scale.

[b] Internal consistency estimates (coefficient alpha) are presented in the diagonal.

TABLE 4

Reliability Estimates for the Measures in the DLOQ

Scale	Initial Measurement		Refined Measurement	
	Coefficient Alpha	Reliability Under CFA	Coefficient Alpha	Reliability Under CFA
Continuous Learning	0.81	0.90	0.71	0.84
Inquiry and Dialogue	0.87	0.91	0.78	0.87
Team Learning	0.86	0.93	0.79	0.87
Embedded Systems	0.81	0.89	0.75	0.85
System Connection	0.84	0.90	0.75	0.84
Empowerment	0.80	0.88	0.68	0.83
Provide Leadership	0.87	0.94	0.83	0.93
Financial Performance	0.74	0.84	0.70	0.79
Knowledge Performance	0.77	0.86	0.64	0.78

Regarding the one-on-one interviews and artifact data, Gibbs (2007) indicated that qualitative research, which includes the three aforementioned forms of data, is increased in reliability by the researcher's approach to ensure the study's consistency with other research projects, as well as different researchers. The researcher followed a strict reliability procedure for the data collection and analysis in this case study to ensure its consistency with other projects and researchers, that reliable data was produced, and that the study was replicable (Yin, 2009). Therefore, the interviews and artifact data, along with Watkins and Marsick's (1997) DLOQ were found to be reliable for data collection in this study.

DATA COLLECTION PROCEDURES

There were three steps involved in the data collection process. First, in the solicitation of study participants, the researcher assigned a numerical code and electronically mailed the 27 official respond- ers that were still employed with the CFD at the time of this study a recruitment letter explaining the study and how their involvement provided much needed insight to the problem (Appendix C, on page XXV). They also received a consent form (Appendix D, on page XXVI) and a confidentiality agreement (Appendix E, on page XXXI), which stated that the participants could withdraw from the study at any time for any reason. With only 27 responders possible for the study, attaining more than 20 of them was a large percentage. If 20 were not attained, the researcher would have provided more infor- mation in a one-on-one meeting with the possible participants to address their concerns regarding participation. Due to the low num- ber of possible participants, 27, the researcher could have performed the study with a smaller sample and still produced rich, in-depth qualitative data due to the use of triangulation with participants and artifact analysis.

Following their agreement to be involved in the study, partici- pants were sent electronic mail with an imbedded link to Kwik- surveys.com, along with detailed instructions on how to complete the questionnaire online. The participants completed the DLOQ (Watkins & Marsick, 1997) online within one week of when they received the email containing the link. Once they completed the DLOQ (Watkins & Marsick, 1997), the data were automatically sent to Kwiksurveys.com for documentation and the researcher logged into the account to identify how many surveys were completed. No personal information was required of the participants to log into the questionnaire. They simply clicked on the embedded link that was electronically mailed to them by the researcher and completed the questionnaire. The researcher sent reminder emails on all seven days that the questionnaire was available to answer by the participants. At the end of seven days, all of the questionnaires were not completed. Therefore, the researcher contacted all of the participants by phone, reminding them of the survey, and allowed them 48 more hours to complete the survey. The researcher did not at any time during the phone call ask the possible participant if they completed the questionnaire. The call was simply a courtesy call to remind them of the link they were electronically sent.

Once the time period expired on the surveys, the researcher randomly selected five participants to participate in a one-on-one interview with the researcher where they answered five open-ended questions developed by three command level officers with over 30 years' of fire service experience, respectively. If one or more of the selected interview participants had not wished to be interviewed, the researcher would have randomly selected an alternate to fill the void. If the alternate decided not to be interviewed, another alternate would have been randomly selected as well. If participants completed the questionnaire but then decided not to partake in the interview, even though the requirements stated everyone was subject to the random selection for the interview, then this information is discussed in Chapters 4 and 5 to allow the reader's knowledge of all participant activity. After all of the questionnaires and interviews were completed, the researcher triangulated the results with artifact analysis from newspaper articles, the CFD's Strategic Plan, CFD standard operating procedures, CFD memos, CFD policies, and other fire service journal articles pertaining to the CFD following June 18, 2007. This enabled the researcher to provide rich, in-depth qualitative data regarding how the CFD learned at the individual, team, and organizational levels following the organizational crisis that ensued beginning June 18, 2007.

The data is stored on the researcher's personal computer and two back up devices for seven years. The devices are locked in a safe in the researcher's home office. The only individual that had access to the Kwiksurveys.com account, where the DLOQ (Watkins & Marsick, 1997) data were stored, was the researcher, and the password to this account was changed monthly to combat any type of fraudulent activity. The artifact analysis is housed in the locked safe in the researcher's home office, where the researcher is the only individual with access to this data as well. The researcher met with the selected interviewees at a location of their choice to ensure that they felt secure in participating. The name of the interviewee, the location or time, and date of the interview were not recorded to ensure total anonymity.

The data was prepared by the researcher by utilizing Kwiksurveys.com to code the responses and create charts and graphs to correlate with the interview results and artifact analysis. The interview questions were also numerically coded by question number and participant, so that the researcher could compare all of the answers to the same question simultaneously, but also have the option of comparing all five of each participant's answers entirely in relation to all five answers of another participant. The artifact data was coded by date, and by the specific type of artifact to allow for organized preparation. For example, a newspaper article or fire service journal article was coded as the date and title of the article. The CFD's Strategic Plan, CFD standard operating procedures, CFD memos, and CFD policies were prepared for data analysis by highlighting the specific areas that were included in the study. These were coded by a numerical system beginning at 0 and proceeding until all of the data was coded.

DATA ANALYSIS PROCEDURES

The specific qualitative coding process for the three sources of data that were used to answer the research questions guiding this study was a process developed by Hatch (2002). This data from the triangulation incorporated the DLOQ (Watkins & Marsick, 1997) completed by all 21 sampled participants, interviews conducted with five randomly selected participants, and artifact data analysis. The artifacts included the CFD's Strategic Plan, CFD memos, CFD policies, CFD standard operating procedures, newspaper articles, and fire service journal articles related to the CFD following June 18, 2007.

Specifically, Hatch's (2002) process consists of the researcher performing nine important data analysis procedures. First, the researcher read the data numerous times to get an idea of the included information and to identify the "analyzable parts" (Hatch, 2002, p. 163). Domains or groups were then created based on specific relationships in the "analyzable parts," with codes then being assigned to the domain or group (Hatch, 2002, p. 163).

The researcher then read the data again to verify the accuracy of the code names and recorded details of the data relationships. Confirmation of the code names was done, as well as a search of the data for specific examples that supported these names. The data analysis was completed utilizing code names where themes were identified across the codes or groups. An outline was then created to highlight the relationships of the themes. Once the relationships of the themes were identified, the researcher selected specific excerpts from the data to add support or indicate examples of the codes included in the outline (Hatch, 2002).

Statistical analysis employed included providing descriptive statistics for the responses from the DLOQ (Watkins & Marsick, 1997). The DLOQ has numerical ratings based on a scale ranging from 1—almost never, to 6—almost always. From these ratings, descriptive statistics were indicated, as well as verbiage to identify how the participants rated each question from 1, almost never, to 6, almost always. Scores of 2, 3, 4, and 5 indicated increasing ratings from 1, almost never, to 6, almost always.

Non-statistical analysis was employed for the interviews and the artifact data. Due to the qualitative nature of the study, the perceptions from the interviewed participants were the focus. The analysis of the interviews and artifact data were not statistical, as the researcher utilized these data sources in triangulation to correlate the results of all three data sources. The data analysis techniques aligned with the research design as utilizing three sources for triangulation allowed for rich, in-depth qualitative data that added to the body of knowledge in the two studied constructs.

ETHICAL CONSIDERATIONS

The anticipated ethical issues surrounding the research in this study centered on participant questionnaires, interviews, and artifact data. All of the participants of the study played some type of role in June 18, 2007. Whether they responded to the first alarm or arrived later to assist, their actions that day have been scrutinized by the public, the media, and numerous investigating agencies.

While many were skeptical to participate, the researcher included an informed consent form (Appendix D, on page XXVI) to explain the methods to ensure complete anonymity, privacy, and confidentiality. Due to the researcher's position in the CFD and the role that the researcher played on June 18, 2007, a clause was included in the informed consent form stating that participants could withdraw from the study at any time if they witness coercion by the researcher or if they identified a conflict of interest. No penalty or harm was placed on a participant if they decided to do so.

By utilizing Kwiksurveys.com, the researcher ensured that the participants' identities were 100% concealed, as they were not required to give any personal information during the DLOQ (Watkins & Marsick, 1997) completion. However, only the researcher knew the five-interviewee identities. The researcher numerically coded the interviews from one to five, with no personal information included.

The researcher followed all of Grand Canyon's Universities IRB board recommendations for the project to ensure ethical participant treatment. During the data collection process, ethical concerns consisted of proper transfer of results to graphs, tables, and charts. The researcher performed two transfers of the results to two different sets of graphs, tables, and charts to ensure that the results were accurately transferred. After the transfers, the two sets were compared and contrasted until both matched identically to the data collected from the DLOQ (Watkins & Marsick, 1997), the interviews, and the artifact data.

To address these ethical considerations from the current study, the researcher utilized The Belmont Report (1979). According to this report, "if there is any element of research in an activity, that activity should undergo review for the protection of human subjects" (The Belmont Report, 1979, p. 1). The current study ensured the protection of human subjects following the three basic ethical principles included in the Belmont Report: respect for persons, beneficence, and justice. The study design, sampling procedures, theoretical framework, research problem, and research questions were all developed focusing on these three important ethical principles.

LIMITATIONS

Limitations of the study included the use of an anonymous questionnaire and interviews. This was first viewed as positive because responders were given the opportunity to participate in the study without fear of retaliation or judgment from present or previous co-workers. However, when an anonymous study is done, answers may not always be truthful. There was no accountability for the answers given in the questionnaires or interviews; therefore, participants may not have been truthful about the events following June 18, 2007.

Another limitation to the study was the use of only responders that officially responded to June 18, 2007 that were still employed with the CFD at the time of this study. According to Lee and Baskerville (2012) a larger sample size allows for greater support of the observations. In the current study, the researcher studied 21 recorded responders of June 18, 2007 that were still employed with the CFD. The number of responders to the incident was much larger than this. Many have moved on to different careers or departments and would not be good candidates for the current study since it focuses on the CFD after June 18, 2007 to the present time at the individual, team, and organizational levels.

The use of internal data for analysis with the questionnaires and interviews also presented a limitation. Members of the CFD, rather than outside agencies, produced this internal data during the change process. Although the researcher utilized outside data in the triangulation to combat this limitation, the limitation was still present.

The existing limitations were unavoidable and were not expected to affect the results negatively. Ioannidis (2007) stated that all research has unavoidable limitations and that the proper discussion and knowledge transfer of these limitations are imperative for progress in the scholarly world. Furthermore, clearly defining limitations was necessary for a better understanding of research results, the improvement of the credibility level, and the indication of potential errors involved (Ioannidis, 2007).

SUMMARY

Shuhui Sophy and Seeger (2012) stated that organizational crises "are those that are recognized as having important lessons for the organization" (p. 75). Weick (1988) stated that organizational crisis is unexpected and endangers organizational goals. When these unexpected types of crises are encountered by high reliability organizations, it makes it difficult for individuals to respond to unstable, unsafe, and rapidly changing environments (Baran & Scott, 2010). James (2007) stated that when an organization is faced with a crisis, the dynamic of the organization changes due to the extreme amounts of stress placed on organizational leaders, employees, and stakeholders.

This chapter included in-depth explanations of the research methodology employed throughout the study, the research design, the sources of data, and the population that was chosen, with an explanation of why they were chosen. Also included in this chapter were discussions regarding the validity and reliability of the research instrument, as well as the reliability of the study as a whole. Finally, data collection and analysis procedures, ethical considerations, and the study's limitations were presented.

In Chapter 4, the results of the aforementioned analyses of the data are presented. Results provided answers to the research questions and described how an organization like the CFD learned from an organizational crisis at the individual, team, and organizational levels. This offers other organizations sound scientific information of an event that has not been rigorously researched in hopes that future firefighters lives will be saved.

CHAPTER 4
Data Analysis and Results

INTRODUCTION

The purpose of this qualitative case study was to explore how the CFD learned from an organizational crisis at the individual, team, and organizational levels. Participants included firefighters from an organization that experienced a critical incident where nine firefighters perished in the line of duty. Data were collected from Watkins and Marsick's (1997) Dimensions of the Learning Organization Questionnaire (DLOQ), interviews, and artifacts to investigate the experiences, events, and strategies employed by the members of the organization, collectively, and as individuals, as they recovered and evaluated their processes as a result of learning.

This chapter presents descriptive data regarding the sample, a detailed description of the data analysis, the study's results, and a summary of the findings. The sample participants and setting of the study are introduced first, followed by data analysis procedures. The results section begins with the presentation of participant responses to Watkins and Marsick's DLOQ (1997). Presentation of the interview responses from the five randomly selected participants and the artifact data follow. The phenomena related to the theories of organizational crisis and organizational learning. The results section presents evidence to support these theories and how they were utilized by an organization to change following a multiple line of duty death (LODD) incident in Charleston, SC on June 18, 2007.

DESCRIPTIVE DATA

The sample utilized in this qualitative case study consisted of 21 firefighters from The City of Charleston Fire Department (CFD) in Charleston, SC that remained employed with the CFD during the conduct of this study. These firefighters officially responded to the June 18, 2007 incident where nine firefighters perished in the line of duty. Participant ages ranged from 25 to 60, with all participants being male. Specific ages will not be given in text or in visual format to ensure anonymity of the participants. The responsibilities of the sample varied, with four rating themselves as general managers, 16 as operations/production employees, and one as a logistics and accounting administrator. The roles of the participants varied, with six being involved in middle management, 11 in a supervisory role, and four in a non-management, technical professional role. Roles differ from responsibilities in that even if a participant's responsibility is as an operations/production employee, they still can be placed in a supervisory role. For example, a captain of an emergency response apparatus is in a supervisory role on that apparatus, but is still considered an operations/production employee because they respond to emergency incidents with the personnel they supervise.

Six of the participants had a high school education, nine had a professional certificate or associate's degree, five had a bachelor's degree, and one participant had a graduate-level degree. The hours expended per month/per participant during non-work hours on work-related learning varied. Specifically, seven sampled participants spent 1–10 non-work hours per month on work related learning, 10 sampled participants spent 11–20 non-work hours per month on work-related learning, three sampled participants spent 21–35 non-work hours per month on work-related learning, and one sampled participant spent 36+ non-work hours per month on work-related learning. Non-work hours spent on work-related learning indicates the time the participants spent doing work-related activities during their off duty time.

Table 5, on page 130 presents the number and percentage of participants according to their primary responsibility, role, educational experience, and hours per month spent off duty on work-related learning. Hours per month spent on work-related learning were included in the table as a descriptor of the participants' involvement in their career during times which they were not compensated for.

TABLE 5

Case Study Participants

Primary Responsibility	Participants
General Management	4 (19%)
Operations / Production	16 (76.2%)
Administration	1 (4.8%)
Role	
Middle Management	6 (28.6%)
Supervisory	11 (52.4%)
Non-Management Technical / Professional	4 (19%)
Educational Experience	
High School Graduate	6 (28.6%)
Certificate or Associates Degree	9 (42.9%)
Undergraduate Degree	5 (23.8%)
Graduate Degree	1 (4.8%)
Hours Per Month Spent Off Duty On Work Related Learning	
0 hours per month	0 (0%)
1 - 10 hours per month	7 (33%)
11 - 20 hours per month	10 (47.6%)
21 - 35 hours per month	3 (14.3%)
36 + hours per month	1 (4.8%)

The raw data were collected from the three sources using triangulation that included the DLOQ (Watkins & Marsick, 1997), interviews, and artifact data, and prepared for analysis. First, the DLOQ (Watkins & Marsick, 1997) results were extracted from Kwiksurveys.com. By utilizing the software included on this website, the researcher was able organize the responses of this Likert-scale survey by each specific question with descriptive statistics given for each response. The responses were then stored on the researcher's computer during data collection of the other two sources.

Next, the interviews took place with the researcher asking the five randomly selected interview participants five open-ended questions. For the random selection, the researcher transcribed all 21 participants' names on separate pieces of 2" x 2" paper, which were folded four times and placed in a 10" x 10" square box. The researcher then shook the box in a clockwise motion ten times and placed the box on a desk. The researcher blindfolded himself, opened the box, and selected five of the 2" x 2" pieces of paper that had the participants' names on them.

After the names were selected, the researcher transcribed each interview separately as they took place and then immediately read the interview responses back to the respective participant to ensure that the raw data that was collected was accurate and that the participant agreed with its inclusion in the study. Once the participant agreed that the information was accurate, the researcher stored the interview responses on the data collection computer while the artifact data was collected.

Finally, the raw artifact data was collected from online sources. The researcher then dissected the artifact data following the process described by Hatch (2002), including the CFD's Strategic plan, CFD standard operating procedures, CFD policies, CFD memos, newspaper articles, and fire service journal articles related to the CFD following June 18, 2007. Once all of the raw data were collected from the artifacts, they were stored on the data collection computer.

The three sources of data, the DLOQ (Watkins & Marsick, 1997) responses, the interviews, and the artifact data, were then organized into the individual, team, and organizational levels. The individual level data were identified with red indicators, the team level with blue, and the organizational level with green. The indicators were simply asterisks placed at the top of each computerized file to allow for easy organization. Some of the raw data included more than one colored asterisk due to that specific piece of data crossing over from one level to another. For example, if data exhibited learning at the individual and organizational level, then there would be two asterisks at the top of the file: one red and one green.

The data analysis technique for this qualitative case study included constructing an explanation to answer the study's research questions that focused on how the CFD learned from organizational crisis at the individual, team, and organizational levels. Hatch's (2002) nine key data analysis procedural steps were utilized to organize data gathered from the sample participants in this study.

The following section describes the nine steps completed. First, the researcher read the data numerous times to get an idea of the included information and to identify the "analyzable parts" (Hatch, 2002, p. 163). During this step, the DLOQ, a Likert-scale survey, was analyzed by each participant's rating at either the lower end of the scale (1 almost never–3) or the upper end of the scale

(4–6 almost always), and by the participant's mean ratings for each respective question (Watkins & Marsick, 1997). The researcher extracted the information from Kwiksurveys.com and utilized the software included on the website, as well as Microsoft Excel, to compute the statistics and means of the results of each question.

These results were then placed in tables in Microsoft Excel as the DLOQ (Watkins & Marsick, 1997) questions, possible ratings, participant responses, and mean ratings. The mean ratings were included in the text, in the tables following each specific part of the DLOQ (Watkins & Marsick, 1997), and in a bar graph included in Appendix F, on page XXXII. The graph identified the question numbers from the DLOQ (Watkins & Marsick, 1997) and the corresponding mean rating for each respective question for all of the sample participants. This allows the reader to refer to the tables and the bar graph for visual descriptors of the mean ratings, as well as the specific wording of the questions included in the DLOQ (Watkins & Marsick, 1997).

Domains (groups) were then created based on specific relationships in the "analyzable parts" (Hatch, 2002, p. 163). Code names were then assigned to the domains. The researcher then read the data again to verify the accuracy of the code names and recorded details of the data relationships. Confirmation of the code names and a search of the data for specific examples that supported these names then took place. The data analysis was then completed utilizing code names. Themes were then identified across the codes or domains. An outline was then created to highlight the relationships of the themes, within and across domains (codes) (Hatch, 2002). The researcher then selected specific excerpts from the data to add support or indicate examples of the codes included in the outline (Hatch, 2002).

The data collection and analysis were completed in a non-evaluative, comprehensible manner. The data consisted of participant responses to Watkins and Marsick's (1997) Dimensions of the Learning Organization Questionnaire (DLOQ), participant interviews utilizing five open-ended questions, and artifact data. Each data source was included in a legend with an assigned abbreviation code. The letter "P" was designated for the participants, as well as a number for each interviewed participant ranging from 1-5. The DLOQ questions were designated "DLOQ" and the interviews were designated as "INTQ" with a correlating number to the specific question (Watkins & Marsick, 1997). The artifact data were designated "AD" with correlating abbreviations for each type of AD. The designation for each data source included the following: newspaper articles (ADNP), the CFD's Strategic Plan (ADSP), CFD standard operating procedures (ADSOP), CFD memos and policies (ADMP), and fire service-related articles (ADFSA). See Table 6, on page 135, which includes assigned abbreviation codes that were utilized in the study.

TABLE 6

Legend

Participants	P
The Dimensions of the Learning Organization Questionnaire	DLOQ
Interviews	INT
Artifact Data	AD
Newspaper Articles	ADNP
The CFD Strategic Plan	ADSP
CFD Standard Operating Procedures	ADSOP
CFD Memos and Policies	ADMP
Fire Service Articles	ADFSA

After reading the data numerous times, the "analyzable parts" included participant answers to the DLOQ (Watkins & Marsick, 1997), interview responses, and artifact data (Hatch, 2002, p. 163). The DLOQ (Watkins & Marsick, 1997) included a ranking system from 1 to 6, where 1 was almost never and 6 was almost always. Scores of 2, 3, 4, and 5 indicated increasing ratings from 1, almost never, to 6, almost always. Furthermore, neutral responses were not possible with the rating system developed for the instrument.

The interviews contained detailed answers to five open-ended questions that the researcher posed to participants individually and in person. The artifact data consisted of published articles, including ADNP, ADSP, ADSOP, ADMP, and ADFSA. Specific relationships were identified in the "analyzable parts" to create domains, which followed Watkins and Marsick's (1997) seven dimensions included in the DLOQ (Hatch, 2002, p. 163). These domains consisted of continuous learning, inquiry and dialogue, team learning, embedded systems, empowerment, system connection, and strategic leadership (Watkins & Marsick, 1997). The code names for these domains included the individual level, team level, and organizational level (Watkins & Marsick, 1997).

To verify the accuracy of the code names and details, the data were read by the researcher and recorded to identify data relationships. The code names were then crosschecked with Watkins and Marsick's DLOQ (1997), and a search of the data for specific examples to support the names was completed. The data analysis was then completed utilizing the code names. During the completion of the data analysis, themes were identified across the codes including learning, listening, and empathy. The themes were utilized to create an outline to highlight relationships within and across the codes (domains). Table 7, on page 138 illustrates the domain names, code names, and descriptions of the domain-codes.

TABLE 7

Domain-Code Names and Descriptions

Domain Name	Code Name	Description
Continuous Learning	Individual Level	Opportunities for growth and education are provided, allowing for learning to occur on the job, and create an organizational culture that supports collective ideas where people listen and inquire others about their views.
Inquiry and Dialogue		
Team Learning	Team Level	Focuses on the encouragement of an environment that is conducive to collaboration, where systems are in place to integrate this collaboration with work.
Embedded Systems		
Empowerment	Organizational Level	The creation of a shared vision through empowerment, the link of the organization to the community, and leadership that utilizes learning strategically.
System Connection		
Strategic Leadership		

Subsequently, selected specific excerpts from the data sources were added to support or to indicate examples of the codes included in the outline (Hatch, 2002). However, outliers were identified in the DLOQ (Watkins & Marsick, 1997). Specifically, one participant rated the DLOQ (Watkins & Marsick, 1997) at the 1-almost never rating more frequently than any of the other participants throughout the questionnaire. Another participant was the exact opposite, rating the DLOQ (Watkins & Marsick, 1997) questions at the 6-almost always rating more frequently than any of the other participants. This indicated two participants that were outside of the normal scope of the mean ratings on all of the DLOQ (Watkins & Marsick, 1997) questions. While this impacted the mean rating of all of the DLOQ (Watkins & Marsick, 1997) responses, they were still included because these were the perceptions of those specific individuals and it was important to include all of the responses to provide a rich, in-depth presentation of the data.

The designs of the DLOQ (Watkins & Marsick, 1997) and the interview questions enabled the researcher to group all of the data into the specific codes stated above. Furthermore, the artifact data enabled the researcher to provide other evidence supporting the codes in the study. For example, DLOQ (Watkins & Marsick, 1997) questions 1 through 13 measured the individual level, questions 14 through 19 measured the team level, and questions 20 through 55 measured the organizational level.

Regarding the interviews, the first interview question related to the individual level, asking participants how the CFD discussed mistakes to allow its members and the fire service to learn from them. The second interview question centered on the team level and how the CFD utilized committees to support the direction of the department. The third question focused on lessons learned from previous emergency and training incidents and pertained to the organizational level. Questions four and five focused on the improvements the participants have made as firefighters and how the CFD's leadership has changed since June 18, 2007, respectively. Once Hatch's (2002) data analysis process was complete, the researcher articulated the data and placed it in chart format for a clearer understanding of the research study's results. See Table 8, on page 141, which indicates the questions from the DLOQ's (Watkins & Marsick, 1997) and interviews that support the codes.

TABLE 8

Codes by Question from the DLOQ and Interviews

Data Source	Individual Level	Team Level	Organizational Level
DLOQ	Questions 1–13	Questions 14–19	Questions 20–55
Interviews	Questions 1 & 4	Question 2	Questions 3 & 5

The researcher utilized a triangulation of sources to increase the construct validity of the study and to create a concentrated line of inquiry (Yin, 2009). Also utilized was a secure electronic database to collect and store all of the data for increased accuracy and reliability (Yin, 2009). The unobtrusive method of triangulation is one of the earliest forms of triangulation and was utilized in this study to "confirm a proposition by two or more independent measurement processes" to reduce the uncertainty of interpretation and increase the reliability of the data collected as well (Webb et al., 1966, p.3).

The presentation of the data includes detailed descriptions of the three codes including the individual, team, and organizational levels from the DLOQ's (Watkins & Marsick, 1997), interviews, and artifact data (Yin, 2009). A possible source of error in these descriptions was identified in the collected data from the 21 participants that completed the DLOQ (Watkins & Marsick, 1997). Since the DLOQ (Watkins & Marsick, 1997) was 100% anonymous, no accountability system to ensure the participants were truthful in their responses was in place. This presents a possible limitation and source of error and may have had a negative effect on the data. The researcher was impacted by the crisis that was studied. However, the researcher followed the data analysis procedures specifically to ensure researcher bias was not present at any time throughout this study. Also, all data was member-checked to ensure the researcher included the data that was expressed by the perceptions of the CFD following June 18, 2007.

RESULTS

The results section focuses on presenting the collected data to answer the study's research questions. These questions consisted of the following: How did an organization like the CFD learn from organizational crisis at the individual level? How did an organization like the CFD learn from organizational crisis at the team level? How did an organization like the CFD learn from organizational crisis at the organizational level? The results section is organized into codes consisting of the individual, team, and organizational levels to allow the researcher to effectively portray participant responses at all three levels and to effectively answer the research questions.

The first code focused upon in the results section of Chapter 4 is the individual level. Following the presentation of the individual level data, the team level, and the organizational level data are presented, respectively. First, from the DLOQ (Watkins & Marsick, 1997), participant responses to questions 1–13 are presented, with responses from interview questions 1 and 4, and artifact data focusing on the individual level following. Next, the team level is presented with DLOQ (Watkins & Marsick, 1997) responses from questions 14–19, responses from interview question 2, and artifact data that focus on the team level of the CFD. Finally, the organizational level is presented with data from participant responses to DLOQ (Watkins & Marsick, 1997) questions 20-55, participant responses to interview questions 3 and 5, and artifact data.

RESEARCH QUESTION 1 (R1):

How did the CFD learn from organizational crisis at the individual level?

DLOQ RESPONSES

The participants answered questions 1–13 from the DLOQ (Watkins & Marsick, 1997) focusing on the individual level of the CFD, with the specifics of each question varying. The 21 participants had the option of answering the questions with a ranking system of 1 to 6, with 1 being almost never and 6 being almost always. For purposes of clarity and presentation, the DLOQ (Watkins & Marsick, 1997) ratings are grouped and referred to as "almost never 1-3" as the lower end of the scale, and "4–6 almost always" as the upper end. Some of the participants did not respond to questions, which was indicated by their blank responses. For further clarity of the results, participant mean ratings are given for each question at the individual level as well. The presentation of the mean ratings for each DLOQ (Watkins & Marsick, 1997) question at the individual level and the upper and lower end of the scale grouping allows the reader to ascertain the participant's perceptions of the CFD at the individual level.

Of the 13 questions contained in the section of the DLOQ (Watkins & Marsick, 1997) that address the individual level, 12 (92%) were scored by more participants in the upper end of the scale (4–6 almost always) rather than the lower end of the scale. These results are as follows: Fifteen of the 21 participants (71%) scored at the upper end of the scale regarding people in the CFD openly discussing mistakes in order to learn from those choices (4.23 mean rating), identifying skills that they needed for future work tasks (4.09 mean rating), giving open and honest feedback to each other (4.00 mean rating), and listening to others' views before speaking (3.76 mean rating). Nineteen of the 21 participants (90%) scored at the upper end of the scale pertaining to people helping each other learn in the organization (5.57 mean rating), with 14 (67%) scoring at the upper end focusing on the encouragement of people to ask why regardless of rank (3.95 mean rating).

Eleven out of the 21 participants (52%) also scored at the upper end of the scale on the following: people ask what others think when stating their views (3.61 mean rating), people are given time to support learning (3.85 mean rating), and people view problems in their work as an opportunity to learn (3.61 mean rating). Thirteen of the 21 participants (62%) scored the DLOQ (Watkins & Marsick, 1997) at the upper end of the scale pertaining to people being rewarded for learning in the CFD (3.52 mean rating), with 17 of the 21 participants scoring at the upper end regarding people treating each other with respect (4.33 mean rating), and spending time building trust with each other (4.33 mean rating). See Table 9, on page 145, which includes the DLOQ (Watkins & Marsick, 1997) individual level questions and the participant mean ratings. For further information on the mean ratings at the individual level, refer to the bar graph in Appendix F, on page XXXII, which lists all of the DLOQ (Watkins & Marsick, 1997) question numbers and their respective mean ratings to provide a visual descriptor for the reader.

TABLE 9

DLOQ Individual Level Questions and Participant Mean Ratings

Questions	Participant Mean Ratings
Do you believe since June 18, 2007...	
1. In my organization, people openly discuss mistakes in order to learn from them?	4.23
2. In my organization, people identify skills they need for future work tasks?	4.09
3. In my organization, people help each other learn?	5.57
4. In my organization, people can get money and other resources to support learning?	3.09
5. In my organization, people are given time to support learning?	3.85
6. In my organization, people view problems in their work as an opportunity to learn?	3.61
7. In my organization, people are rewarded for learning?	3.52
8. In my organization, people give open and honest feedback to each other?	4.00
9. In my organization, people listen to others' views before speaking?	3.76
10. In my organization, people are encouraged to ask "why" regardless of rank?	3.95
11. In my organization, whenever people state their view, they also ask what others think?	3.61
12. In my organization, people treat each other with respect?	4.33
13. In my organization, people spend time building trust with each other?	4.33

Note: Scale: 1 almost never - 6 almost always

INTERVIEWS

From the five open-ended questions asked to five randomly selected participants, INTQ1 and INTQ4 focused on the individual level of the organization. Sampled participant responses to these two questions are presented below with subheadings INTQ1 and INTQ4. Since INTQ2 pertains to the team level and INTQ3 and INTQ5 pertain to the organizational level, their responses are not presented with the individual level responses. They are presented with their respective codes.

INTERVIEW QUESTION 1 (INTQ1)

How does the CFD discuss mistakes to allow its members and the fire service to learn from them?

Participant 1 (P1) stated:

"Now every day is a learning experience with the use of critiques and training to help everyone improve on their mistakes."

Participant 2 (P2) indicated:

"The CFD is more open about mistakes now, whereas before, we didn't take the opportunity to learn from mistakes." Finally, P2 indicated prior to June 18, 2007 there was "more criticism and the department was ridiculed when mistakes happened."

Participant 3 (P3) stated:

"Critiques after fires are only good if we point out mistakes. A

146

lot of stuff is left out. We have to call out mistakes. Critical Incident Reviews (CIR) help, but the routine critiques don't go anywhere. The CIR's go on the computer for everyone to learn from, whereas, the critiques don't." P3 continued, "Discussions of mistakes are more in depth now than they were, and learning from mistakes has gotten better."

Participant 4 (P4) stated:

"There are several things that we do now. After any major call or fire, a critique or discussion takes place with all of the companies that were involved. You can Monday morning quarterback yourself, which is not a negative thing. Chiefs are there to let you know where you made mistakes and what you did well. It is an open forum that is unadulterated with no backlash or headhunting. This is an effort to make everyone better." P4 went on to state, "During CIR's, personnel that were not on scene analyze the incident to allow outside people to talk about the good and bad in the incident. This is then published for everyone to read. This is a great forum for learning."

Participant 5 (P5) stated:

"We have done a poor job of doing it ourselves. We have not done a full open discussion on a national stage. The department hired committees to perform independent reviews, which were connected to the recommendations stemming from June 18, 2007, but they were not completely unbiased." P5 continued, "We have not done it justice. Every day we don't do it, the lessons are reduced. We were labeled as an ignorant backwoods department, but we weren't that far off. We just didn't have the proper tactics. There are still major departments operating the way we did. We just thought we were better than we actually were."

INTERVIEW QUESTION 4 (INTQ4)

How have you learned as a firefighter since June 18, 2007?

Participant 1 (P1) recalled:

Going into the new chief's office and "there were blank sheets of paper all over the walls for action plans, training, apparatus, fire station overhauls, money plans, raises, etc. to make us better firefighters." P1 continued that prior to June 18, 2007 all "I had was 1152," a basic firefighting course, whereas now, "I have FF1 and FF2," which are more advanced firefighting courses. P1 went on to state, "The increased training has allowed me to take numerous incident command courses to improve my incident command skills. These courses make me think more about the big picture, such as positioning of apparatus, safety, and accountability. Before it was balls to the wall, get there first, no accountability, no size up, no crew integrity. Now we are well on our way to an established department."

Participant 2 (P2) stated:

"I now take more courses and do anything to improve my knowledge and the department. I want to be an example and to show the guys this is what we need to be doing. Not a day goes by that I don't look at an article or website to improve myself. I am more visual and hands on now and the job awareness and thinking has improved since the fire."

Participant 3 (P3) stated:

"I learned from our mistakes. I am more aware of what is going on around the country. All of the classes have made me smarter and more responsible." P3 continued, "I have also improved from the Officer Development Program, fire ground simulation, and command training."

Participant 4 (P4) indicated that he believed:

"The greatest tool for learning is the environment. If an environment is conducive to learning, people learn. The previous environment was not good. The training division is doing a great job with this, where they make you do it until it is right in a positive manner. There may be remedial training, but the atmosphere is better. Today there is no fear of not knowing something or asking questions." P4 expressed, "Our environment has blossomed. I can't count how many new things I have learned and improved upon. I have a lot more patience, I'm not as reckless, and I now take my time to make a sound decision. We don't jump right into harm's way anymore; we now have a calculated manner in our operations. We see more now."

Participant 5 (P5) expressed:

"I learned I wasn't invincible. My knowledge of commercial structures and building construction has increased. I learned gallons per minute, and IQ is important and that firefighting is more to do with what is between the ears. My mental aspect and thought process has improved." P5 continued, "I realize that it is ok to be defensive on a fire. Just make the decision and live with it. The firefighters may hate me now, but if they can still call me an SOB in 50 years because they survived their career, I did my job."

ARTIFACT DATA

To finalize the triangulation of the study, the researcher collected artifact data (AD) from different sources to add depth to individual level learning in the CFD. These sources consisted of newspaper articles (ADNP), the CFD's Strategic Plan (ADSP), CFD standard operating procedures (ADSOP), CFD memos and policies (ADMP), and fire service articles (ADFSA). Refer to Table 5, on page 130 from the Data Analysis Procedures section of Chapter 4.

ARTIFACT DATA STRATEGIC PLAN (ADSP)

Expressing learning at the individual level, according to ADSP, the CFD has "created and delivered" the Officer Development Program that has been recognized by the South Carolina Fire Academy (SCFA) for certification, in which all current officers have received the specialized training (CFD Strategic Plan, 2013). Furthermore, the CFD has a published training matrix with the requirements for promotion, incorporated computer based command officer training, trained all line personnel in Rapid Intervention Team procedures, trained the members to the FFII level, sent personnel to the National Fire Academy (NFA) for leadership training, improved and increased the length of recruit training to allow new firefighters to be trained at the FFII level and beyond, adopted the "Everyone Goes Home Program" from the National Fallen Firefighters Foundation to promote firefighter safety, and has created opportunities for members to attend fire service conferences to increase their training and personal development (CFD Strategic Plan, 2013).

ARTIFACT DATA STANDARD OPERATING PROCEDURES (ADSOP)

Data from ADSOP regarding post incident reviews states that the purpose of a post incident review "is to help identify ways that the CFD can improve safety and efficiency at emergency incidents. A properly conducted post incident review allows all responding personnel to voice recommendations, concerns, and frustrations, which might otherwise serve no worthwhile purpose" (CFD SOP 201.07, 2009, p. 1).

Furthermore, the Post Incident Review Form is not intended to be used as a scorecard, but only as a guide so that all major aspects of the incident are reviewed and documented. A properly completed Post Incident Review Form will serve as a good starting point for a Critical Incident Review (CIR) work group and may lead to the purchase of additional/better equipment, additional training, or SOP's (CFD SOP 201. 07, 2009, p. 1).

ADSOP 101.2, 101.3, and 101.4 pertain to the promotions of personnel to higher level positions in the CFD consisting of engineer, captain, and battalion chief, respectively. The purpose of these policies "is to establish a process for competitive promotion" (CFD SOP 101.2, 2013, p. 1). All of the policies have a specific promotional matrix for each of the designated positions. For example, to be eligible for promotion to battalion chief, according to ADSOP, personnel must have 4 years or more of consecutive service as a captain and 11 years of consecutive service with the CFD. Also, "Effective 2014, all candidates must have satisfactorily completed" Incident Command System 300, Incident Command System 400, Incident Command for High Rise, Leadership II, NFPA Fire Officer II, Response to Terrorism, Incident Safety Officer, and the Officer Development Program. ADSOP goes on to state, "Effective 2014, all candidates for battalion chief must have a minimum of thirty (30) college credit hours in a degree program to include an English 100 series and a Math 100 series (CFD SOP 101.4, 2013, p. 2). Candidates that were promoted prior to 2014 must complete the curriculum listed "within 24 months of promotion to successfully complete probation" (CFD SOP 101.4, 2013, p. 2).

ARTIFACT DATA MEMOS AND POLICIES (ADMP)

According to ADMP, the CFD utilizes a variety of strategies including mentoring, training, direct support, incident simulation, and incident experience to develop and support the growth of organizational leaders (CFD Memo Career Development, 2009). "The CFD strives to be a leadership organization," therefore, it is important that expectations of members are defined so that they can more effectively map out their career paths (CFD Memo Career Development, 2009, p. 1). The memo goes on to state that national standards have been created to assist departments in this type of development for every job responsibility and level in the fire service. "The CFD must use those standards as guidance for our organizational vision" (CFD Memo Career Development, 2009, p. 1).

The CFD utilizes tuition reimbursement for its employees. According to ADMP, The City of Charleston "encourages and supports" the development of its personnel with educational funding that increases their "effectiveness and contribution" towards departmental goals (CFD Memo Tuition Reimbursement, 2013, p. 1). The City of Charleston will pay a portion of an employee's tuition, which is related to the current job of an employee or to assist in potential job advancement based on their grade in the course. For example, if the employee makes an A or B in a course, they are reimbursed 85% of the tuition, up to $2000 per year. Making a C or PASS awards the employee 75% of tuition, up to $2000 per year, and making a D, F, or FAIL does not award the employee any reimbursement funds (CFD Memo Tuition Reimbursement, 2013).

Once CFD personnel complete their degrees, whether an associate's, bachelor's, or master's degree, they are awarded a 5% raise per degree. Therefore, an associate's degree will award personnel 5%, a bachelor's degree will award them another 5%, for a total of 10%, and a master's degree will award an additional 5%, totaling 15%. Firefighters, assistant engineers, engineers, captains, battalion chiefs, and assistant chiefs are awarded these increases in salary. Deputy chiefs and the fire chief are not eligible for this raise in salary, but are eligible for the reimbursement (CFD Memo Tuition Reimbursement, 2013).

ARTIFACT DATA FIRE SERVICE ARTICLES (ADFSA)

Includes data from different sources around the fire service. First, according to Sendelbach (2012), five years after the fire that claimed nine City of Charleston firefighters, Chief Thomas Carr ensured the CFD and its personnel are "rising from the ashes of tragedy to become a recognizable symbol of fire service excellence" (p. 1). He stated that the fire that occurred at the Sofa Super Store in 2007 has offered "countless lessons" for all to learn from. There isn't a better way to honor the nine firefighters that were lost "than to learn from this incident, and train others to do the same" (Sendelbach, 2012, p. 1).

Another piece of ADFSA comes from Foskett (2012), who interviewed the deputy chief of operations of the CFD. One of her interview questions asked the deputy chief how he feels about the progress that the CFD has made and if he is happy with the changes that have taken place. His response was as follows:

"I can't recall another department in the country that has absorbed and implemented as many changes as the CFD in such a short period of time. I think the department has made tremendous progress in a very compressed time period. The hurdles the members have had to overcome and the processes they have had to learn were extraordinary. The bar is constantly being moved to the next level of achievement here, with everything from a fireboat coming to the department to higher levels of education, but the members continue to meet the challenges and achieve goals in an admirable fashion" (p. 2).

Foskett (2012) also asked the deputy chief what he would like to see that the fire service and the CFD's personnel learn from the event that took place on June 18, 2007. The deputy chief replied:

"June 18, 2007 was a horrific tragedy for the CFD. The American fire service would do well to take that specific incident and use it as a template for assessing its own performance and capability. The CFD is an organization filled with extraordinary individuals. Many of them have worked tirelessly to honor the loss of the

Nine by taking every opportunity to improve their knowledge, skills, and abilities. I think the membership learned that adversity can be overcome with perseverance, their professionalism can carry them anywhere they want to go, and they are every bit as good as the best fire department anywhere" (Foskett, 2012, p. 3).

RESEARCH QUESTION 2 (R2):
How did the CFD learn from organizational crisis at the team level?

DLOQ RESPONSES

The participants answered questions 14–19 from the DLOQ (Watkins & Marsick, 1997) focusing on the team level of the CFD, with the specifics of each question varying. The 21 participants had the option of answering the questions with a ranking system of 1 to 6, with 1 being almost never and 6 being almost always. For purposes of clarity and presentation, the DLOQ (Watkins & Marsick, 1997) ratings are referred to as "almost never 1-3" as the lower end of the scale, and "4–6 almost always" as the upper end. For further clarity of the results, participant mean ratings are given for each question at the team level as well. Some participants did not respond to questions, as indicated in the results where responses for all 21 participants were not recorded. The presentation of the mean ratings for each DLOQ (Watkins & Marsick, 1997) question at the team level and the upper and lower end of the scale grouping allows the reader to ascertain the participant's perceptions of the CFD at the team level.

Of the six possible questions from the DLOQ (Watkins & Marsick, 1997) relating to the team level, three (50%) of them were scored in the upper end of the scale (4–6 almost always), while participants scored 3 (50%) at the lower end of the scale (almost never 1–3). Upper end of the scale scoring pertained to the following questions: "Do you believe since June 18, 2007 . . ." in my organization, teams treat members as equals, regardless of rank, culture, or other differences (3.42 mean rating), "Do you believe since June 18, 2007 . . ." in my organization, teams focus both on the group's task and how well the group is working (4.52 mean rating), and "Do you believe since June 18, 2007 . . ." in my organization, teams revise their thinking as a result of group discussions or other information collected (4.23 mean rating). Specifically, results indicated that 11 (52.4%), 18 (85.7%), and 14 (67.7%) out of the 21 participants, respectively, scored these questions at the upper end of the scale (4–6 almost always).

Scoring at the lower end of the scale by participants at the team level was indicated on the following questions: "Do you believe since June 18, 2007 . . ." in my organization, teams have the freedom to adapt their goals as needed (3.35 mean rating), "Do you believe since June 18, 2007 . . ." in my organization, teams are rewarded for their achievements as a team (2.80 mean rating), and "Do you believe since June 18, 2007 . . ." in my organization, teams are confident that the organization will act on their recommendations (2.90 mean rating). Specifically, results indicated that 11 (52.4%), 16 (76.2%), and 13 (62%) participants, respectively, scored these questions pertaining to the team level of the CFD at the lower end of the scale (almost never 1–3).

See Table 10, on page 158, which includes the DLOQ (Watkins

& Marsick, 1997) team level questions and the participant mean ratings. For further information on the mean ratings at the team level, refer to the bar graph in Appendix F, on page XXXII, which lists all of the DLOQ (Watkins & Marsick, 1997) question numbers and their respective mean ratings to provide a visual descriptor for the reader.

TABLE 10

DLOQ Team Level Questions and Participant Mean Ratings

Questions	Participant Mean Ratings
Do you believe since June 18, 2007...	
14. In my organization, teams have the freedom to adapt their goals as needed?	3.35
15. In my organization, teams treat members as equals, regardless of rank, culture, or other differences?	3.42
16. In my organization, teams focus both on the group's task and how well the group is working?	4.52
17. In my organization, teams revise their thinking as a result of group discussions or information collected?	4.23
18. In my organization, teams are rewarded for their achievements as a team?	2.80
19. In my organization, teams are confident that the organization will act on their recommendations?	2.90

Note: Scale: 1 almost never - 6 almost always

INTERVIEWS

From the five open-ended questions asked of five randomly selected participants, INTQ2 focused on the team level of the organization.

INTERVIEW QUESTION 2 (INTQ2)

How does the CFD utilize committees to support the direction of the department?

Participant 1 (P1) stated:

"Before the fire there were no committees. Now there is a committee for everything. For example, uniforms, apparatus, and personal protective equipment." P1 continued, "Committees now drive the department to a certain degree, with the chief and the deputy chief having the ultimate decision. Committees are there to direct them."

Participant 2 (P2) stated:

"Before the fire there were no committees. It was always the same people being selected. This didn't always make for the right choices." P2 went on to state, "Now committees are used more and they do give us more insight, but committees as a whole need to be more random because it seems it is always the same people volunteering. We should randomly select, rather than get volunteers."

Participant 3 (P3) stated:

"Before the fire, there was one group of people that decided everything. Now there are a lot of committees, but they aren't broad enough. They're usually only a handful of people that are on them and they don't meet as often as they should." P3 continued, "Committees definitely drive the department more now than they use to, but could be improved."

Participant 4 (P4) stated:

"There have been several committees brought to light since the fire, such as the uniform and apparatus committees. The committees give everyone the opportunity to voice their opinion about the direction of the department. Before the fire we would not be involved in the decisions." In addition, P4 indicated, "We have a voice now and personally, I think they work because it gives the guys with boots on the ground the feeling of making an important decision for the direction of the department."

Participant 5 (P5) expressed:

"Before June 18th there was a singular approach with micro-management. The decisions were made based on a political platform and a propensity toward a low impact upon the city's budget." P5 also stated, "Now we utilize committees, and they are a good approach 99% of the time. In order for the department to go a long way, we must go as a group, rather than one person. This empowers more members of the department to become involved and increases their buy in."

ARTIFACT DATA

To further align triangulation to the qualitative case study methodology of this study, artifact data (AD) was gathered from a variety of sources to add greater depth to team level learning in the CFD. These sources consisted of newspaper articles (ADNP), the CFD's Strategic Plan (ADSP), CFD standard operating procedures (ADSOP), CFD memos and policies (ADMP), and fire service articles (ADFSA). Refer to Table 5, on page 130 from the Data Analysis Procedures section of Chapter 4 for additional representations.

ARTIFACT DATA STRATEGIC PLAN (ADSP)

Since 2007, The City of Charleston has created committees and working groups throughout the organization. They consist of the Health and Safety Committee, Apparatus and Equipment Committee, Training Committee, Standard Operating Procedure Committee, Recruitment Committee, Fireboat Committee, Radio Working Group, Truck Company Working Group, Deputy Chief's Advisory Committee, Promotional Working Groups, and Critical Incident Review Working Groups. Another group organized following 2007 was the Peer Support group, focusing on firefighter behavioral health. This team of firefighters is available 24 hours a day for all personnel if they are in need of support (CFD Strategic Plan, 2013, p. 42).

ARTIFACT DATA STANDARD OPERATING PROCEDURES (ADSOP)

According to ADSOP, the CFD has established an awards program to recognize the outstanding performance of units (teams) and individuals (CFD SOP 116.01, 2013, p. 5). Units are recognized with a Unit Citation, which is a certificate issued to a company (team) by the fire chief for actions taken "that demonstrated courage, ingenuity, or placed the department in a favorable light with the community" (CFD SOP 116.01, 2013, p. 5). Unit Citations have the potential of being issued multiple times during a one-year period to different companies (team) at the fire chief's discretion. Members of the department may complete the Awards Program Nomination Form to nominate a member or unit (team) for an award.

ARTIFACT DATA MEMOS AND POLICIES (ADMP)

According to ADMP, in 2009, members of the organization were solicited to create a committee to develop and administer new promotional exams for engineer and captain promotions. Specifically, ADMP stated that the purpose of the memo was "to solicit members interested in assisting with developing the exams" (CFD Memo Promotional Exam Writers, 2009, p. 1). This process involved Exam Development Teams that were essential components to creating an exam process that was "relevant to the rank" (CFD Memo Promotion Exam Development Teams, 2009, p. 1).

ARTIFACT DATA NEWSPAPER ARTICLES (ADNP)

ADNP adds more depth to the team level with data that highlights an incident in April 2013 where crews from the CFD "hit the building hard and fast" but with a "coordinated plan, with the aid of other departments and with an eye toward safety that resulted in everyone getting out before things got bad" (Smith & Elmore, 2013, p. A1). The mayor of the city "was even more effusive, saying fire crews did an excellent job saving a piece of downtown's rich fabric without incurring a single injury or allowing the fire to spread to neighboring properties. They did an amazing job" (Smith & Elmore, 2013, p. A1).

More ADNP from the April 2013 incident indicated, "Fire crews were on scene within four minutes and were soon joined by a small army of reinforcements. Automatic and mutual aid was one of the improvements introduced after the Sofa Super Store, and crews from area fire departments now regularly train together and respond to each other's calls as a matter of course, with all operating from the same playbook" (Smith & Elmore, 2013, p. A4).

RESEARCH QUESTION 3 (R3):
How did the CFD learn from organizational crisis at the organizational level?

DLOQ RESPONSES

The participants answered questions 20–55 from the DLOQ (Watkins & Marsick, 1997), focusing on the organizational level of the CFD with variation on the specifics of each question. However, questions 44–55 specifically focused on measuring learning organization results at the organizational level. The data will be presented at this level in two groups, questions 20–43, and questions 44–55 for greater succinctness and transparency in presentation of the results.

The 21 participants had the option of answering the questions with a ranking system of 1 to 6, with 1 being almost never and 6 being almost always. To indicate results with greater clarity, the DLOQ (Watkins & Marsick, 1997) ratings are referred to as "almost never 1–3" as the lower end of the scale, and "4–6 almost always" as the upper end. For further clarity of the results, participant mean ratings are given for each question at the organizational level as well. The presentation of the mean ratings for each DLOQ (Watkins & Marsick, 1997) question at the organizational level and the upper and lower end of the scale grouping allows the reader to ascertain the participant's perceptions of the CFD at the organizational level. Some participants did not respond to all of the questions, which was indicated in the results with the total number of responses not equal to a total of 21.

From the possible 24 questions (20–43) in the first group of the organizational level, 18 (75%) were scored by more participants in the upper end of the scale (4–6 almost always), leaving 6 (25%) scoring at the lower end (almost never 1–3). Specifically, participant responses indicate scoring at the upper end of the scale on the following:

- People get needed information at any time quickly and easily (3.90 mean rating).
- The organization maintains an up-to-date database of employee skills (4.19 mean rating).
- The organization makes its lessons learned available to all employees (4.33 mean rating).
- The organization measures the results of the time and resources spent on training (3.85 mean rating).
- The organization recognizes people for taking initiative (3.80 mean rating).
- The organization invites people to contribute to the organization's vision (4.09 mean rating).
- The organization gives people control over the resources

they need to accomplish their work (4.00 mean rating).

- The organization builds alignment of visions across different levels and work groups (3.65 mean rating).
- The organization encourages people to think from a global perspective (3.45 mean rating).
- The organization encourages everyone to bring the customer's views into the decision making process (3.85 mean rating).
- The organization works together with the outside community to meet mutual needs (4.71 mean rating).
- People are encouraged to get answers from across the organization when solving problems (3.95 mean rating).
- Leaders generally support requests for learning opportunities and training (4.19 mean rating).
- Leaders share up to date information with employees about competitors, industry trends, and organizational directions (3.90 mean rating).
- Leaders empower others to help carry out the organization's vision (4.00 mean rating).
- Leaders mentor and coach those they lead (4.14 mean rating).
- Leaders continually look for opportunities to learn (3.85 mean rating).
- Leaders ensure that the organization's actions are consistent with its values (3.95 mean rating).

Six of the first 24 questions (20–43) at the organizational level were scored at the lower end of the DLOQ (Watkins & Marsick, 1997) scale (almost never 1–3). These questions pertained to the following:

- The organization's use of two-way communication on a regular basis, such as suggestion systems, electronic bulletin boards, and town hall / open meetings (3.35 mean rating).
- The organization's creation of systems to measure gaps between current an expected performance (3.52 mean rating).
- Allowing people choices in their work assignments (3.38 mean rating).
- The support of employees who take calculated risks (3.19 mean rating).
- Helping employees balance work and family (2.85 mean rating).
- The impact that decisions have on employee morale (2.14 mean rating).

See Table 11, on page 167, to view the DLOQ (Watkins & Marsick, 1997) organizational level questions and the participant mean ratings. For further information on the mean ratings at the organizational level, refer to the bar graph in Appendix F, on page XXXII, which lists all of the DLOQ (Watkins & Marsick, 1997) question numbers and their respective mean ratings to provide a visual descriptor for the reader.

TABLE 11

DLOQ Organizational Level Questions and Participant Mean Ratings

Questions	Mean Ratings
Do you believe since June 18, 2007...	
20. My organization uses two-way communication on a regular basis, such as suggestion systems, electronic bulletin boards, town/hall open meetings?	3.35
21. My organization enables people to get information at any time, quickly and easily.	3.90
22. My organization maintains an up-to-date database of employee skills?	4.19
23. My organization creates systems to measure gaps between current and expected performance?	3.52
24. My organization makes its lessons learned available to all employees?	4.33
25. My organization measures the results of time and resources spent on training?	3.85
26. My organization recognizes people for taking initiative?	3.80
27. My organization gives people choices in their work assignments?	3.38
28. My organization invites people to contribute to the organization's vision?	4.09
29. My organization gives people control over the resources they need to accomplish their work.	4.00
30. My organization supports employees who take calculated risks?	3.19
31. My organization builds alignment of visions across different levels and work groups?	3.65

32. My organization helps employees balance work and family?	2.85
33. My organization encourages people to think from a global perspective?	3.45
34. My organization encourages everyone to bring the customers' views into the decision making process?	3.85
35. My organization considers the impact of decisions on employee morale?	2.14
36. My organization works together with the outside community to meet mutual needs?	4.71
37. My organization encourages people to get answers from across the organization when solving problems?	3.95
38. In my organization, leaders generally support requests for learning opportunities and training?	4.19
39. In my organization, leaders share up to date information with employees about competitors, industry trends, and organizational directions?	3.90
40. In my organization, leaders empower others to help carry out the organization's vision?	4.00
41. In my organization, leaders mentor and coach those they lead?	4.14
42. In my organization, leaders continually look for opportunities to learn?	3.85
43. In my organization, leaders ensure that the organization's actions are consistent with its values?	3.95

Note: Scale: 1 almost never–6 almost always

The second group of questions (44–56), measured learning at the organizational level of study consideration. Of the 12 questions included in this section, seven were scored by participants at the upper end of the scale (4–6 almost always) and 4 were scored by participants at the lower end of the scale (almost never 1–3), while one question was answered evenly at both ends of the scale. Some participants did not complete all of the questions, which was indicated in the total number of responses not totaling 21, even though 21 total participants completed the research study.

Results indicate that participants scored the CFD at the upper end of the scale on the DLOQ (Watkins & Marsick, 1997) (4–6 almost always) on specific organizational performance topics compared to the previous year (2012). Their responses refer to a greater average productivity per employee than indicated previously (4.09 mean rating), a more timely span of response time for customer complaints (3.90 mean rating), greater customer satisfaction (4.38 mean rating), more new products or services (4.57 mean rating), more skilled workers (4.80 mean rating), increased spending devoted to technology and information processing (4.28 mean rating), and an increase in the number of individuals learning new skills (4.90 mean rating).

Participants scored at the lower end of the DLOQ (Watkins & Marsick, 1997) (almost never 1–3) on four out of the 12 (33.3%) learning organization measurement questions. These included the following questions: "Do you believe since June 18, 2007 . . ." in my organization, time to market for products and service is less than last year (3.00 mean rating)?, "Do you believe since June 18, 2007 . . ." in my organization market share is greater than last year (3.00 mean rating)?, "Do you believe since June 18, 2007 . . ." in my organization, the cost per business transaction is greater than last year (2.84 mean rating)?, and "Do you believe since June 18, 2007 . . ." in my organization, the number of suggestions implemented is greater than last year (3.14 mean rating)? Specifically, 13 out of the 21 (62%) participants scored the first two aforementioned questions at the lower end of the scale, with 14 (67%) and 11 (52.4%) scoring the latter two questions in this manner, respectively. One question in this group was addressed evenly on both ends of the scale, with 10 (50%) participants each scoring in this manner and one not completing the question. The question read as follows: "Do you believe since June 18, 2007 . . ." in my organization, return on investment is greater than last year (3.50 mean rating)?

See Table 12, on page 171, for the remainder of the DLOQ (Watkins & Marsick, 1997) organizational level questions and the participant mean ratings. For further information on the mean ratings at the organizational level, refer to the bar graph in Appendix F, on page XXXII, which lists all of the DLOQ (Watkins & Marsick, 1997) question numbers and their respective mean ratings to provide a visual descriptor for the reader.

TABLE 12

DLOQ Organizational Level Questions and Participant Mean Ratings

Questions	Participant Mean Ratings
Do you believe since June 18, 2007...	
44. In my organization, return on investment is greater than last year?	3.50
45. In my organization, average productivity per employee is greater than last year?	4.09
46. In my organization, time to market for products and services is less than last year?	3.00
47. In my organization, response time for customer complaints is better than last year?	3.90
48. In my organization, market share is greater than last year?	3.00
49. In my organization, the cost per business transaction is less than last year?	2.84
50. In my organization, customer satisfaction is greater than last year?	4.38
51. In my organization, the number of suggestions implemented is greater than last year?	3.14
52. In my organization, the number of new products or services is greater than last year?	4.57
53. In my organization, the percentage of skilled workers compared to the total workforce is greater than last year?	4.80
54. In my organization, the percentage of total spending devoted to technology and information processing is greater than last year?	4.28
55. In my organization, the number of individuals learning new skills is greater than last year?	4.90

Note: Scale: 1 almost never - 6 almost always

INTERVIEWS

From the five open-ended questions posed to five randomly selected participants, INTQ3 and INTQ5 focused on the organizational level of the CFD.

INTERVIEW QUESTION 3 (INTQ3)

How does the CFD ensure that all employees are aware of lessons learned from previous emergency and training incidents?

Participant 1 (P1) stated:

"We now have Critical Incident Reviews (CIR), and training, training, and more training."

Participant 2 (P2) indicated:

"The CFD is more aware that training is important. Hindsight is always 20/20. Before, people thought you couldn't be taught anything out of a book. It all had to be hands on. Education was not going to make you on this job back then." P2 continued, "We are more conscious and aware that mistakes we made have changed our thought patterns. We are now assessing rather than reacting. If it doesn't improve, we don't do it. There is much more thought now rather than before the fire."

Participant 3 (P3) stated:

"Critical Incident Reviews (CIR) are done and put on the computer for everyone to learn." P3 continued, "We have increased training, and are more aware of near miss programs now than before the fire." Additionally, P3 added, "There is room for improvement in the discussion of mistakes on daily incidents . . . this would have made the department better if we would have done this before the fire."

Participant 4 (P4) responded:

"Before the fire there were no Critical Incident Reviews (CIR) or critiques after incidents. Now the Critical Incident Reviews (CIR) and critiques help. We can listen to the call from the dispatcher's point of view to realize our mistakes or things we did well. This is a great training tool and learning environment for some that may not go on as many calls as others to improve their size up and tactics." P4 also stated, "I know mistakes will always be made, but as long as you are not bashed, you can learn from it."

Participant 5 (P5) indicated:

"Recruit school starts with and ends with lessons from June 18th. People complain about how much we talk about the event, but it is a consistent reminder that it could be you. If we aren't reminded with the faces on the wall and the names on the truck, personnel may get the superman attitude." P5 added, "The ultimate irony is recruit school. We train them for six months to be followers only to be released to the line to be leaders." P5 continued, "You make them invincible during recruit school, but put a chink in their armor before they graduate so they know they aren't."

INTERVIEW QUESTION 5 (INTQ5)

How has the CFD's leadership changed since June 18, 2007?

Participant 1 (P1) stated:

"There is more accountability on each individual firefighter now, classes have increased, and physical fitness has improved." P1 added, "Before the fire, it depended on who you were and what you did wrong. Now everyone is held accountable for his or her actions in a consistent manner. This was a much-needed change for the department. I did not agree with how the old administration handled things, but I was here too long to go anywhere else. I did not have the qualifications and education to go to another department because only a select few got to take courses." P1 closed by stating, "We are now a more uniform department in leadership."

Participant 2 (P2) indicated:

"Before the fire we had a pretty dynamic leader. He was more personal, more outgoing, and more involved in the community. Our leadership today is not as involved with the community as previous leaders were. Today they are more involved in running the department. This has caused us to go on the wrong end of customer service. We still need the community outreach because this helps the department in the long run. Now leadership is lacking in this aspect." P2 added, "Our leadership training now is more proactive than before. We used to be told that we don't need classes and that a book can't put out a fire. Now we have improved on the delivery and the quality of the training. This has encouraged our people to get more training."

Participant 3 (P3) described:

"The CFD as a business." This participant further stated, "Leadership is worried about money out, but safety is number 1." P3 added, "We are heading in a great direction to allow us to keep up with national standards, but when leadership changes you go in two different directions sometimes." P3 continued, "It is hard to believe in 6 years we have done this much change." In closing, P3 stated, "Leadership has moved away from interaction with the guys. Everything is different now."

Participant 4 (P4) stated:

"Where do you start? Leadership has totally changed for the men and women of the CFD. Promotions are now done with a fair system based on testing, practical exercises, and management tools. This is directly related to the leader's decision to improve this." P4 continued, "The leadership change has allowed me to grow as a firefighter and as a leader. Their style has definitely helped the CFD for the better."

Participant 5 (P5) expressed:

"Everything has changed. We are a unique public agency because upper level management has changed their whole philosophy. You don't see that in government a lot. We are now so flexible. Our reflex time is so fast." P5 added, "Our new philosophy and tradition is the ability to change and strive for perfection. We are an east coast fire department as close to a west coast fire department there is."

ARTIFACT DATA

To finalize the triangulation of the study, the researcher collected artifact data (AD) from different sources to add depth to organizational level learning in the CFD. These sources consisted of newspaper articles (ADNP), the CFD's Strategic Plan (ADSP), CFD standard operating procedures (ADSOP), CFD memos and policies (ADMP), and fire service articles (ADFSA). Refer to Table 5 from the Data Analysis Procedures section of Chapter 4, on page 130 for more.

ARTIFACT DATA STRATEGIC PLAN (ADSP)

ADSP indicates that since 2007 new positions have been created in the CFD. These include three deputy chiefs, a logistics officer, a safety officer, an increased number of training instructors, a public information officer / community educator, administration assistants, and additional captain and engineer positions. Additionally, an entire department, the fire marshal's division, was also established, raising the number of personnel from 246 in 2007 to 318 in 2013 (CFD Strategic Plan, 2013).

The fire marshal division was created in July of 2010, with the hiring of a fire marshal that is responsible for public education / community outreach, fire code enforcement, fire plan review, permitting, and fire investigations. Two deputy fire marshals, two assistant fire marshals, and one inspector were added to the team, with other inspectors from The City of Charleston's building department transferring into the division as inspectors as well. The Fire Investigation Team (FIT) was created to allow regional and internal participation in the division. A Peninsula Fire Investigation Task force was then created, as well as the establishment of fire plan review, a permitting process, standard public education curricula, and community outreach programs (CFD Strategic Plan, 2013).

ADSP also indicated changes to the operations division. These changes included four person minimum staffing, 45 minute Self Contained Breathing Apparatus (SCBA), gear lockers, improved station uniforms, large diameter hose and appliances, 12 Rapid Intervention Team packs, new extrication equipment, thermal imaging cameras for all apparatus, lapel microphones and radio straps for all portable radios, positive pressure ventilation fans (PPV), rabbit tools, rope rescue equipment, search ropes, ventilation saws, rescue jacks, vehicle stabilization equipment, command and safety vests, an accountability system, an increased size of response package to front-load incidents with the proper resources, and rapid egress systems for each firefighter. To allow all of these resources to be utilized effectively, the Consolidated Dispatch Center was developed and implemented as well (CFD Strategic Plan, 2013).

According to ADSP, the CFD special teams were retrained to a higher level. Specifically, the Hazardous Materials Response Team was updated and retrained to the International Association of Firefighters' 80-hour program. The Urban Search and Rescue Team was updated and retrained to standards set by the South Carolina Fire Academy and the International Association of Firefighters. The Marine Division was then formed and a fireboat was purchased to provide service to the coastal areas. The fireboat "Louis Behrens" was placed into service in November of 2012 (CFD Strategic Plan, 2013, p. 40).

The CFD's apparatus also improved since 2007, with a more innovative style of command vehicle chosen to support all incident command situations and the retrofitting of all engine companies with 1¾" attack lines. Some engine companies were also retrofitted with cross lay hose storage, reflective material, and air conditioning. An air and light truck and rehabilitation truck and trailer were added to the fleet, with many of the department's engines being replaced with new innovative apparatus. The CFD has also purchased a tiller truck and a hazardous materials response unit to increase the quality of service. The hazardous materials response unit was made possible by funds from a grant (CFD Strategic Plan, 2013).

The administration of the CFD also showed changes according to ADSP, including an improved hiring and promotional process, and the development of a regionally adopted Safe Structural Firefighting Standard Operating Procedure (SOP). In order to follow this SOP, a cooperative response for automatic and mutual aid was developed. ADSP also indicated that policies, procedures, orders, and memos were added to a central computer database to allow all members of the department ease of access, with a second personal computer being placed in all fire stations to support the effort of the members in their higher learning endeavors (CFD Strategic Plan, 2013).

Grants received by the CFD were also highlighted in ADSP with six grants in total. First, in 2008, the CFD was awarded a grant for diesel exhaust extraction systems, rapid egress escape systems, gear lockers, and extrication equipment. Also in 2008, the CFD was awarded the Staffing for Adequate Fire and Emergency Response (SAFER) grant for 24 firefighter positions. In 2009, the department was awarded the Fire Act Grant for 1¾" attack hose, new nozzles, portable monitors, stabilizer struts for truck companies, automatic external defibrillators, and a rehabilitation truck with the equipment to coincide.

Also in 2009, the Federal Emergency Management Agency (FEMA) awarded the CFD with a grant for a fireboat. Then, in 2010, True North Gear funded the CFD with a grant for nationally recognized subject matter experts on "Big Box" fires to instruct the organization. Finally, in 2011, the CFD was awarded the Fire Act Grant for the highly recognized International Association of Firefighters' Fireground Survival Training (CFD Strategic Plan, 2013).

ARTIFACT DATA STANDARD OPERATING PROCEDURES (ADSOP)

According to ADSOP, rules and regulations were put in place to assist in preserving order and maintaining a higher standard of service to the community. All personnel were expected to use their skills, knowledge, training, and education to ensure exemplary conduct. Section 6.1.1 of ADSOP 102.01 states, "personnel are expected to do their work and conduct themselves competently and professionally when on duty, to accept responsibility for their own conduct, and to show personal and professional integrity at all times" (CFD SOP 102.01 Code of Conduct and General Orders, 2013, p. 1). ADSOP 102.01 goes on to state that personnel will follow all provisions of the SOP's, as well as the department, state, and city policies. If personnel do not do so, they will be held accountable for their actions and may be disciplined.

Further research of ADSOP indicates that the purpose of SOP

115.08 Transfer Policy was to provide "a method for the reassignment of an employee from one duty assignment to another" and that "personnel will normally serve a minimum of two years in a duty assignment" (CFD SOP 115.08 Transfer Policy, 2009, p. 1). It further stated that it was the responsibility of the employee to complete a Transfer Request Form if they desired a transfer, which would then be forwarded through the chain of command. Chief officers considered these requests from personnel with less than two years in an "assignment for extenuating circumstances" (CFD SOP 115.08 Transfer Policy, 2009, p. 1).

According to ADSOP, the purpose of CFD SOP 115.01 (2009) Staff Scheduling and Electronic Roster was to "establish shift staffing documentation continuity between all work shifts and ensure proper personnel attendance for payroll records" (p. 1). ADSOP also stated that the new staff scheduling and electronic roster would streamline the organization's scheduling process, with the forecast of shift scheduling being three shifts out from the day of duty. Projection forms were stored in a shared file on the computer database to ensure all chiefs had access to scheduling and that the roster was filed with the on duty assistant chief by 0900 the day of operation.

ADSOP indicates that the CFD began new programs for community outreach and education. One of these programs was the After the Fire Neighborhood Canvas, where the neighborhood in the "immediate vicinity of a significant fire event" was canvased by on duty CFD firefighters to "provide educational information to the neighborhood and assist citizen's return to a sense of normalcy" (CFD SOP 606.04 After the Fire Neighborhood Canvas, 2011, p. 1). During the canvas, department members attempted "to visit each home in the immediate area of an incident" offering "to test, change batteries, or install smoke alarms" (CFD SOP 606.04 After the Fire Neighborhood Canvas, 2011, p. 2). If the citizen was not home upon visitation, the firefighters left approved fire safety documentation at the main door.

Another community program developed by the CFD in 2011 was the Fire in the Streets (FITS) program. According to ADSOP, the purpose of this program was to improve the safety of the citizens through proactive activities. The main goal of the program was one on one interaction between CFD firefighters and the citizens of the community to exchange valuable life safety information. This program allowed for direct information through handouts and discussions to the citizens, and offered them the opportunity to ask important questions or invite firefighters into their homes to review a potential problem. In the event that serious hazards were discovered, they were reported directly to the fire marshal for review (CFD SOP 606.05 Fire in the Streets, 2011).

A bag was assembled for each station to utilize during the FITS program. This bag included 10 smoke alarms, one cordless drill, one small drill, one pack of wall anchors, one universal screwdriver, 12 9-volt batteries, 20 fire safety bulletins, 20 home escape plans, three sets of self-adhesive numbers, one clipboard, smoke detector request forms, and writing pens. This equipment allowed the CFD to offer the best community risk reduction and education program possible (CFD SOP 606.05 Fire in the Streets, 2011).

ADSOP also had an impact on the CFD's organizational operations during emergency incidents. According to the CFD SOP 200.01 (2012) Standard Operating Procedure for Safe Structural Firefighting, the purpose was to "describe fire department policy regarding risk assessment and safety management while setting standard apparatus dispatch response assignments, company personnel assignments, and command guidelines . . . in order to enhance operational safety, effectiveness, and efficiency" (p. 3). The SOP applied to all personnel operating on an emergency scene from area departments that utilized mutual and automatic aid. The goal of the document was to provide the safest possible working environment for the membership of the CFD and surrounding organizations. Each member was ordered to be accountable for his or her own safety and minimize risks to others (CFD SOP 200.01, 2012, p. 3).

Following emergency incidents, the CFD participated in post-incident reviews. According to ADSOP, the purpose of incident reviews were to identify ways that the CFD could improve their safety and efficiency during emergency incidents. The CFD used three specific methods to do this: a tailboard review / hot wash, an incident critique, and a Critical Incident Review (CIR). A tailboard review / hot wash was held at the emergency scene prior to personnel's release, but after all responders had a full rehabilitation cycle. An incident critique was done at a centrally located fire station as soon as possible following the emergency incident, with all available personnel that responded to the incident included in the review (CFD SOP 201.07 Post Incident Review, 2009).

The final method of post-incident analysis was a Critical Incident Review (CIR). A work group was assigned by the fire chief or the deputy chief of operations to complete the analysis. This was the most in-depth type of analysis and was completed when the work group published a report to the department with all names and unit numbers anonymous (CFD SOP 201.07 Post Incident Review, 2009).

Awards are a part of the CFD with a program to honor personnel who currently serve in the department and preserve the excellent performance by dedicated members from previous generations.
ADSOP indicates that peer nomination for awards and department recognition are important components "to promoting positive morale within the workforce" (CFD SOP 116.01 Awards Program, 2013, p. 1). All members of the department were eligible for
an award, commendation, medal, service bar, or unit citation. Any
member of the department was allowed to submit a nomination for
consideration. The awards committee created by the deputy chief of
administration convened to select the winners of all of the yearly
awards. Specific awards included the Medal of Valor, the Medal of
Gallantry, the EMS Life Saving Award, the New Life Award, Chief
Officer of the Year, Captain of the Year, Engineer of the Year, Firefighter of the Year, the Community Outreach Award, the Longevity
Award, the Excellence in Service Certificate, the Fire Chief's Award
of Excellence, a Unit Citation, and Commendation (CFD SOP 116.01
Awards Program, 2013, p. 6).

ARTIFACT DATA MEMOS AND POLICIES (ADMP)

ADMP indicated that the CFD brought in a nationally recognized
speaker to educate the department on crew resource management
and the near-miss reporting system. CFD Memo 09-7 (2009) stated
that a great opportunity was presented when a dynamic and power-
ful speaker from the Montgomery County, Maryland Fire Rescue
Service visited the CFD for an all-day event. The department was

informed that it needed "to make a good showing" because if the interest was not there, it would reduce other training "opportunities in the future due to poor attendance" (CFD Memo 09-7, 2009, p. 1). The ADMP went on to state that the training was free to all, with lunch being provided for everyone.

Communication was addressed in ADMP that indicated the CFD provided all personnel with a private email address in 2009 to improve communications, to ensure all personnel had access to information when they needed it, and to provide privacy of that information. ADMP went on to state that "honest, respectful, two-way communication" was critical to the organization's success and that each individual was responsible for checking their assigned email at least once per shift when they were on duty (CFD Memo 09-13, 2009, p. 1). Individuals were to be knowledgeable of communication that occurred since their previous shift, and if it was found that they were not, then they were held accountable (CFD Memo 09-13, 2009).

ADMP indicated that changes were made to the CFD's incident reporting in the Firehouse software program. CFD Memo 11-9 (2011) stated that in order to standardize the entered narrative information into Firehouse, a new auto-generated template was added. This template assisted the Incident Commander in providing a clear and concise synopsis of the emergency incident. CFD Memo 11-9 (2011) went on to state that often times, the Firehouse report may be the only information that an insurance company or homeowner receives; therefore, it was imperative that the information was accurate, and provided a satisfactory overall account of the emergency (p. 1).

According to ADMP, response issues were also addressed. Specifically, CFD Memo 13-08 indicated that CFD companies reported difficulties exiting the station on local alarm assignments when responding Alpha mode. It added that the situation had caused numerous near misses and extended the response time of companies. To decrease these occurrences and ensure a timely response, all units dispatched to automatic alarms were allowed to "display emergency lights and sound audible warning devices to provide for safe egress from the station" (CFD Memo 13-08, 2013, p. 1). These devices were to be utilized for up to two intersections past the fire station and then discontinued for all units besides the first due unit.

ADMP indicated that staffing is a critical component of fire-fighter safety and operational efficiency in the organization. CFD Memo 13-09 (2013) stated that the overtime costs for 2013 were outpacing the budgeted funds, where in previous years the organization was able to make up the difference due to savings from vacancies. It went on to state that the organization could not continue to incur the high level of spending, maintain four-person staffing, and remain within the allotted budget. Therefore, modifications were made to the leave policy, including reducing the maximum number of sick leave spots, the cancellation of the personal sick leave program, and specific instructions for available leave slots and disability (CFD Memo 13-09, 2013).

Further research of ADMP indicated that due to a recent gap in the CFD's driver/operator class regarding driving hours of potential promotees to the position of assistant engineer, two specified paths for promotion were documented in an interim memo until a permanent policy was more thoroughly developed. CFD Memo 13-15

(2013) stated that firefighters were allowed to take one of two specific paths to attain the promotion of assistant engineer. Path one included the completion of an assistant engineer application, with a copy of the candidates class E license and 10 year driving record. The candidate then had to successfully complete the CFD driver/operator course and 50 hours of driving time, with 10 hours of cone drills, 20 hours during the daytime in all battalions, and 20 hours at night in all battalions as well (CFD Memo 13-15, 2013).

Path 2 began similarly to Path 1, with the candidate turning in an application with a copy of their class E license and 10 year driving record. They were then allowed to train in-station utilizing the CFD Driver / Operator Handbook as a guide. During this time, they were also required to complete 50 hours of driving time broken down exactly as it was in Path 1. Once the candidate completes either path, the training division will schedule an appointment to complete the two-part test of driving and pumping the apparatus. If they were successful at both components, then they were promoted to assistant engineer. If they were unsuccessful, they were allowed to retest in 30 days (CFD Memo 13-15, 2013).

ARTIFACT DATA FIRE SERVICE ARTICLES (ADFSA)

Moving to ADFSA, research indicated that the Charleston Fire Department has made "sweeping changes in an effort to ensure a similar event never occurs again" (Devone-Pacheco, 2010, p. 2). Further ADFSA indicated that on the 6-year anniversary of the Sofa Super Store fire, the National Fallen Firefighters' Foundation released a documentary on the CFD entitled *Charleston 9: The*

Ultimate Sacrifice. Pieper (2013) stated in her article on the documentary that the department's change is depicted in every aspect of its "operations, from recruit classes who ring a bell at the end of each day to remind them of their successful training and the importance going home to their families, to new equipment, to modern-day incident command, to a renewed focus on continual training." One firefighter in the documentary was recorded as saying, "I'm still coming to win, but I'm doing it in a smarter way" (Pieper, 1013). The late chief responsible for the unprecedented change in the department stated, "This will be a place not known for the Sofa Super Store fire, but for what came after" (Pieper, 2013, p. 2).

ADFSA also provided data from one of the members of The CFD's Post Assessment and Review Team following the event on June 18, 2007. Sendelbach (2013) stated that the department has "undergone monumental organizational changes, and put forth a culture of safety that will unquestionably be a model for fire departments around the world" (p. 1). He added a clear message has been spoken and spoken loudly: "Change has come" (Sendelbach, 2013, p. 3).

More ADFSA indicated a follow-up article by Devone-Pacheo (2012) on her 2010 look at the CFD. She stated that the CFD had a new normal, including 100% participation in state fire academy training, the development and participation of an 80-hour Officer Development Program, training the entire department to the FFII level, rapid intervention training, a more innovative recruit school, and the awarding of a grant for the International Association of Firefighters (IAFF) Fire Ground Survival School to be hosted at the CFD's training facility. In Devone-Pacheo's (2012) article, a CFD member commented on the IAFF program stating that it ensured the CFD was training to the national standard. In closing, he expressed that "we want to teach our own people the newest techniques, but we also want to make it so that our people can go out and teach others" (p. 4).

ADFSA from the leader of The CFD Post Assessment and Review Team stated during an interview with Foskett (2012) that the CFD is now a much different organization, with the most important change demonstrated in the overall orientation of the organization. The leader further added, "countless positive changes have occurred, and continue to occur, because the leadership has taken the department in the right direction and the members have enthusiastically adopted new concepts and adapted to change" (Foskett, 2012, p. 2). During the interview he was asked how he felt about the progress and changes that have been made in the CFD. He stated that he is "convinced that the department has exceeded expectations in terms of radical and rapid change." He continued, "The good news is that the CFD is in good condition and moving in the right direction with positive backing from City Hall" (Foskett, 2012, p. 4).

In an interview with the last officer to exit the Sofa Super Store fire, he was asked what he saw as the most significant changes in the CFD. The officer replied:

"The culture is moving toward a safer response. The job is still the job, someone has to go put the fires out, but we're changing the technology now, trying to work smarter, not harder. There's a lot more manpower on the trucks, and we're responding in a safer more organized, methodical manner" (Devone-Pacheco, 2010, p. 2).

ADNP from Smith and Elmore (2013) stated that a recent response to a structure fire in the historic district of Charleston, SC "demonstrated the fruits of hard lessons learned in the aftermath of the June 2007 Sofa Super Store blaze that killed nine city firefighters" (p. A1). The article stated that the interior crews fought the fire as "long as they could before evacuating for safety reasons around 1:44 am . . . In time the roof collapsed, but all crews were at a safe distance by then, fighting the blaze from a defensive posture" (Smith & Elmore, 2013, p. A4). The article went on to state that the department has dedicated itself and worked hard after June 18, 2007 to honor its traditions, while continuing to improve its operations. The fire chief stated, "That was good, smart firefighting" (Smith & Elmore, 2013, p. A4).

THEMES

From the data analysis, themes were identified across the codes and domains, including learning, listening, and empathy, which were used to develop a conceptual model. Thus, across the code's individual level, team level, and organizational level, learning, listening, and empathy were apparent. See the outline below created to highlight the relationships of the themes within and across the domains (codes) following Hatch's (2002) data analysis process. Following the outline, refer to the conceptual model (Figure 1) developed to express the findings in the outline and to identify the themes that were developed from the domains in the research study. Furthermore, the outline below includes bullet points from the data collected by the

DLOQ (Watkins & Marsick, 1997), the interviews, and artifact data to support each theme that were identified over the domains. These bullet points are also included in the conceptual model to specify the results of the study that were apparent across the domains and that led to the identification of the three themes: learning, listening, and empathy.

OUTLINE OF RELATIONSHIPS OF THE THEMES, WITHIN AND ACROSS THE DOMAINS (CODES)

Learning, within and across the individual level, team level, and organizational level.

- Work skills are identified
- People help each other learn
- Lessons learned from mistakes
- Increased training and education
- Improved policies, procedures, and memos
- Artifact data identifying learning

Listening, within and across the individual level, team level, and organizational level.

- Increased communication
- Others' views are sought in the decision-making process
- Personnel have a voice now
- Discussions of problems and mistakes
- Personnel views are listened to now
- Time is spent between personnel to build more trust

Empathy, within and across the individual level, team level, and organizational level.

- Everyone is given an opportunity to collectively improve the CFD
- Empowerment
- Respect
- Leaders give personnel time and resources to learn
- Equal treatment regardless of rank
- Alignment of the organizational vision

As indicated above, the themes identified from the data analysis included listening, learning, and empathy across the individual level, team level, and organizational level. The individual level was comprised of the domain's continuous learning and inquiry and dialogue, the team level was comprised of the domains of team learning and embedded systems, and the organizational level was comprised of the domains of empowerment, system connection, and strategic leadership. These three levels were highlighted in the organizational learning that took place in the CFD following June 18, 2007. From the organizational learning indicated in this study, the three aforementioned themes were identified, with specific examples of the themes in and across all of the codes and domains presented throughout the research (Hatch, 2002). The conceptual model below presents a picture of organizational learning based on the thematic analysis of the data.

FIGURE 1.

Conceptual Model.

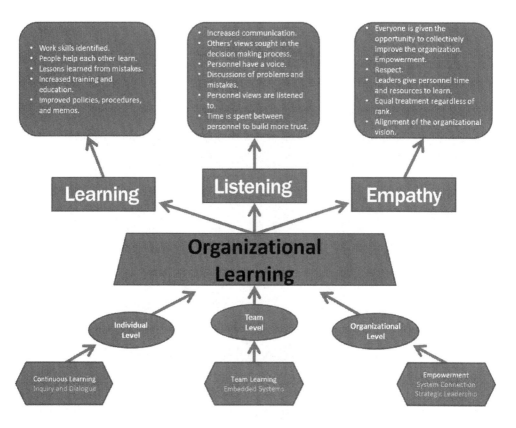

SUMMARY

The data collection and analysis of this qualitative case study was conducted to answer the following research questions. First, the overarching question was: How were organizational processes and employee behaviors changed following a crisis? This overarching question was answered by the guidance of the research sub-questions, which included the following:

R1: How did the CFD learn from organizational crisis at the individual level?

R2: How did the CFD learn from organizational crisis at the team level?

R3: How did the CFD learn from organizational crisis at the organizational level?

The data analysis consisted of the 21 sampled participants' DLOQ (Watkins & Marsick, 1997) responses, the five randomly selected participant interviews, and artifact data consisting of the CFD's Strategic Plan, CFD standard operating procedures, CFD memos and policies, newspaper articles, and fire service articles focusing on the CFD following June 18, 2007. The triangulation of the data allowed for a rich, in-depth understanding of the CFD following June 18, 2007.

The themes identified from the data analysis included listening, learning, and empathy across the individual level, team level, and organizational level. The individual level was comprised of the domains of continuous learning and inquiry and dialogue, the team level was comprised of the domains of team learning and embedded systems, and the organizational level was comprised of the domains of empowerment, system connection, and strategic leadership. These three levels were highlighted in the organizational learning that took place in the CFD following June 18, 2007. From the organizational learning indicated in this study, the three aforementioned themes were identified, with specific examples of the themes in and across all of the codes and domains presented throughout the research (Hatch, 2002). Refer to the Figure 1, which indicates the domains, levels, and themes from this research study.

Following Hatch's (2002) final step in the data analysis procedures, the researcher selected specific excerpts from the data to indicate examples of the levels included in the outline consisting of the individual level, team level, and organizational level. These excerpts identified how organizational processes and employee behaviors changed following a crisis. Specifically, DLOQ (Watkins & Marsick, 1997) data from the individual level indicated more open discussions of mistakes, identification of future work tasks, and open and honest feedback. Further individual level data indicated that personnel listen to others' views before speaking, help each other learn, are encouraged to ask why, ask what others think before stating their view, are given time to support learning, view problems in their work as an opportunity to learn, are rewarded for learning, treat each other with respect, and spend time building trust with each other.

Individual level data from interviews indicated, "Now every day is a learning experience" (P1). P2 added, "The CFD is more open about mistakes now, whereas before, we didn't take the opportunity to learn from mistakes." P3 continued, "Discussions of mistakes are more in depth now than they were, and learning from mistakes has gotten better." P4 stated, "I can't count how many new things I have learned and improved upon."

Artifact data from an interview with the deputy chief of operations of the CFD indicated an example of the individual level as well. He stated:

"The CFD is an organization filled with extraordinary individuals. Many of them have worked tirelessly to honor the loss of

194

the Nine by taking every opportunity to improve their knowledge, skills, and abilities. I think the membership learned that adversity can be overcome with perseverance, their professionalism can carry them anywhere they want to go, and they are every bit as good as the best fire department anywhere" (Foskett, 2012, p. 3).

Examples of the team level from the DLOQ (Watkins & Marsick, 1997) indicated that teams treat members as equals, regardless of rank, culture, or other differences, teams focus both on the group's task and how well the group is working, and teams revise their thinking as a result of group discussions or other information collected. Further data indicating examples of the team level included interview responses. P1 stated, "Before the fire there were no committees. Now there is a committee for everything." P2 added, "Now committees are used more and they do give us more insight." P4 indicated, "We have a voice now and personally I think they work because it gives the guys with boots on the ground the feeling of making an important decision for the direction of the department."

Artifact data exemplifying the team level indicated that since 2007, The City of Charleston Fire Department has created committees and working groups throughout the organization. They consist of the Health and Safety Committee, Apparatus and Equipment Committee, Training Committee, Standard Operating Procedure Committee, Recruitment Committee, Fireboat Committee, Radio Working Group, Truck Company Working Group, Deputy Chief's Advisory Committee, Promotional Working Groups, and Critical Incident Review Working Groups (CFD Strategic Plan, 2013).

Specifically, further artifact data exemplifying the team level indicated that in 2009 members of the organization were solicited to create a committee to develop and administer new promotional exams for engineer and captain promotions (CFD Memo Promotional Exam Writers, 2009, p. 1).

Examples of the organizational level from the DLOQ (Watkins & Marsick, 1997) indicated that people obtain needed information at any time quickly and easily, an up-to-date database of employee skills is maintained, lessons learned are available to all employees, people are recognized for taking initiative, people are invited to contribute to the organizations vision, and people are encouraged to get answers from across the organization when solving problems. Furthermore, leaders generally support requests for learning opportunities and training, mentor and coach those they lead, continually look for opportunities to learn, and ensure that the organization's actions are consistent with its values. Further data indicating examples of the organizational level included interview responses. P1 stated, "We now have Critical Incident Reviews (CIR), and training, training, and more training." P2 indicated, "The CFD is more aware that training is important." P3 continued, "We have increased training, and are more aware of near miss programs now than before the fire."

Regarding leadership in the CFD, P1 stated, "We are now a more uniform department in leadership." P2 added, "Our leadership training now is more proactive than before." P4 continued, "The leadership change has allowed me to grow as a firefighter and as a leader. Their style has definitely helped the CFD for the better." Finally, according to P5, "Everything has changed. We are a unique public agency because upper level management has changed their whole philosophy."

Artifact data exemplifying the organizational level indicated that numerous new leadership positions were created in the CFD, as well as the creation of the fire marshals division. Also, additional equipment was added since June 18, 2007 consisting of 45-minute Self Contained Breathing Apparatus (SCBA), large diameter hoses and appliances, Rapid Intervention Team packs, new extrication equipment, Thermal Imaging Cameras, positive pressure ventilation fans (PPV), rabbit tools, rope rescue equipment, search ropes, ventilation saws, vehicle stabilization equipment, an accountability system, and an increased size of response packages to front-load incidents with the proper resources, to name a few. The CFD's apparatus also improved since 2007, with the purchase of a more innovative style of command vehicle, new engines, new aerials, a hazardous materials response unit, a rehab truck and trailer, and an air and light truck (CFD Strategic Plan, 2013).

Further artifact data exemplifying the organizational level indicated that following emergency incidents, the CFD participated in post incident reviews. The purpose of incident reviews were to identify ways that the CFD could improve their safety and efficiency during emergency incidents. Communication was addressed organizationally as well. In 2009, all personnel were provided with a private email address to improve communications and to ensure all personnel had access to important information (CFD Memo 09-13, 2009). Artifact data exemplified the organizational level further from research completed by one of the members of The CFD's Post Assessment and Review Team following the event on June 18, 2007.

Sendelbach (2013) stated that the department has "undergone monumental organizational changes, and put forth a culture of safety that will unquestionably be a model for fire departments around the world" (p. 1). He added that a clear message has been spoken and spoken loudly: "Change has come" (Sendelbach, 2013, p. 3).

From the analysis, results indicated that the CFD has learned from the organizational crisis that ensued following June 18, 2007. In response to R1, results indicated that the CFD learned following organizational crisis at the individual level, however, there were areas identified that needed improvement. In relation to R2, results indicated that the CFD learned from organizational crisis at the team level, however, there were areas identified that needed improvement as well. Finally, in response to R3, results indicated that the CFD learned from organizational crisis at the organizational level, however, there were areas identified that needed improvement.

The findings reflect key information as they address the problem identified in the study of how it is not known how an organization like the CFD learned from organizational crisis at the individual, team, and organizational levels. These findings are presented more in Chapter 5, where the researcher provides a summary of the study, findings and conclusions from the study, the study's implications, and recommendations for future research and practice.

CHAPTER 5

Summary, Conclusions, and Recommendations

INTRODUCTION

The purpose of this qualitative case study involved how an organization like The City of Charleston Fire Department (CFD) learned following an organizational crisis at the individual, team, and organizational levels. The research questions that guided the study asked: How did the CFD learn from organizational crisis at the individual level? How did the CFD learn from organizational crisis at the team level? How did the CFD learn from organizational crisis at the organizational level? To answer the study's research questions, the researcher collected and analyzed the 21 sampled participants' responses to Watkins and Marsick's (1997) Dimensions of the Learning Organization Questionnaire (DLOQ), interviews (INT) from five randomly selected participants, and artifact data (AD) comprising the CFD's Strategic Plan (ADSP), CFD standard operating procedures (ADSOP), CFD memos and policies (ADMP), newspaper articles (ADNP), and fire service articles (ADFSA). This was completed to ensure triangulation was performed inclusive of a focused line of inquiry (Yin, 2009).

The study is important because many organizations have faced or will face crises that lead to grave consequences. Additionally, organizational crises are becoming more inevitable due to the increase of complexity and technology-based processes in organizations (Lin et al., 2006). Furthermore, crises are bound to occur, more specifically in large, complex systems stemming from the external environment and organizational malfunctions (Perrow, 1984; Rochlin, 1991). Public service organizations are comprised of these complex systems in their response to the external environment. In addition to these elements, the presence of organizational malfunctions relate to the potential for organizational crises.

The research findings of this study indicated how an organization learned at the individual, team, and organizational levels following an organizational crisis stemming from multiple line-of-duty deaths on June 18, 2007 in Charleston, SC. These findings can be utilized by other organizations to identify areas needing potential changes to alleviate a possible organizational crisis, or to respond following an organizational crisis stemming from a major event or a LODD incident. Also, the research findings offer organizations research that can provide for the development of programs to increase levels of education, training, and leadership. The findings of this study identified patterns between personnel who officially responded to the multiple LODD incident on June 18, 2007, in conjunction with what current literature identified as characteristics of organizational crisis and organizational learning. Moreover, this study appeared to be the first qualitative case study focused on how an emergency services organization learned following an organizational crisis with a multiple LODD incident at the individual, team, and organizational levels.

A comprehensive summary of this qualitative case study is provided in Chapter 5. Specifically, this Chapter includes how the results pertain to what is known in the current literature on organizational crisis and organizational learning, how the research questions were answered, and the depth and quality that the theoretical framework was supported by data collection and analysis.

SUMMARY OF THE STUDY

The qualitative case study stemmed from an exhaustive review of the literature and questions focusing on how organizational learning can be utilized to prevent or combat organizational crisis. Watkins and Marsick's (1997) DLOQ was the foundational theoretical model for this research study. Furthermore, the case study by James (2007) and exploring current literature on organizational crisis and organizational learning impacted the researcher's interest in and approach to this research. In addition, given the researcher's experience in a multiple LODD incident that led to an organizational crisis, the review of the aforementioned literature sparked the researcher's interest to complete a study that could benefit organizations during their time of organizational crisis, as well as prevent this type of occurrence altogether. During the time of organizational crisis in the CFD, the researcher reflected upon how the experience of June 18, 2007 had negatively impacted so many lives. Following this reflection period, the researcher became involved in higher learning endeavors to ensure positive comes out of that tragic day when nine firefighters perished. Furthermore, could ascertaining how an organization like the CFD learned from organizational crisis at the individual, team, and organizational levels influence other organizations to change their operations for safer, more innovative practices to combat organizational crisis and prevent it altogether? These ideas and questions led to an extensive review of the literature and guided the researcher during the proposal and dissertation process.

Hatch's (2002) nine key data analysis procedural steps were utilized to complete this qualitative methodology and case study design. The data analysis consisted of responses of the 21 sampled participants to Watkins and Marsick's (1997) DLOQ, interviews (INT) with five randomly selected participants, and artifact data (AD) comprised of the CFD's Strategic Plan (ADSP), CFD standard operating procedures (ADSOP), CFD memos and policies (ADMP), newspaper articles (ADNP), and fire service articles (ADFSA). The DLOQ (Watkins & Marsick, 1997) consisted of questions that focused on an organization at the individual, team, and organizational levels. Specifically, questions 1 to 13 measured at the individual level, questions 14 to 19 measured at the team or group level, and questions 20 to 55 measured at the organizational level.

The interviews (INT) were completed next with five randomly selected sampled participants. The first interview question related to the individual level, asking participants how the CFD discusses mistakes to allow its members and the fire service to learn from them. The second interview question centered on the team level and how the CFD utilizes committees to support the direction of the department. The third interview question focused on lessons learned from previous emergency and training incidents, and pertained to the organizational level. Questions four and five were directed toward the improvements the participants have made as firefighters and how the CFD's leadership has changed since June 18, 2007. Artifact data (AD) was then utilized to finalize the triangulation of data sources and provide greater depth to the research study. During the triangulation of data sources, the researcher utilized predetermined themes from Watkins and Marsick's DLOQ (1997) consisting of the individual, team, and organizational levels.

According to Watkins and Marsick (1997), the individual level consists of continuous learning, inquiry, and dialogue. This level was described as providing opportunities for growth and education, allowing for learning to occur on the job, and to create an organizational culture that supports collective ideas where people listen and inquire about others' views. The team level consisted of team learning and embedded systems, and was described as focusing on an environment that is conducive to collaboration, where systems are in place to integrate collaboration with work. The organizational level consisted of empowerment, system connection, and strategic leadership, described as the creation of vision through empowerment, community involvement, and leadership that utilizes learning strategically.

Construct validity through triangulation was established from the researcher synthesizing all of the available data (Yin, 2009). The description and presentation of the DLOQ (Watkins & Marsick, 1997) responses, interview responses, and artifact data coincided to provide a cross-sectional understanding of the organizational crisis following June 18, 2007, which allowed the researcher to present a summary of the study's findings, as well as the conclusions of the study. The convergence of these data sets merged to indicate the experience of how the CFD utilized organizational learning in the CFD to combat organizational crisis following the multiple LODD's on June 18, 2007. The results indicated that the CFD learned at the individual, team, and organizational levels, specifically. Furthermore, results also indicated that there are still areas in the CFD at the individual, team, and organizational levels that need improvement.

SUMMARY OF FINDINGS AND CONCLUSION

To allow for a clear and concise understanding of how an organization like the CFD learned from organizational crisis at the individual, team, and organizational levels, the researcher presented a summary of the findings in chronological order, beginning with the DLOQ (Watkins & Marsick, 1997) responses, moving to the interviews, and ending with the artifact data (Yin, 2009). Inductive logic was then utilized to ensure the study's findings were grounded in prior literature and research to allow for the presentation of possible conclusions (Creswell, 2009). The summary of findings and conclusion section is organized into the identical themes from Chapter 4, inclusive of the individual, team, and organizational levels.

SUMMARY OF FINDINGS

During the data collection, different views were expressed on The Dimensions of the Learning Organization Questionnaire (DLOQ) (Watkins & Marsick, 1997), the interviews, and the artifact data. However, there were specific examples that attributed to answering the research questions of this study. These examples lend to the findings of the research.

The DLOQ (Watkins & Marsick, 1997) responses indicated that

learning at the individual level was present in the CFD regarding the open discussion of the mistakes that would offer opportunities for learning and the identification of skills needed for future work tasks. Additionally, responses indicated that CFD personnel help each other learn, are given time to support learning, and view problems in the work environment as an opportunity to learn. Furthermore, the DLOQ (Watkins & Marsick, 1997) indicated that CFD personnel give open and honest feedback to each other, listen to others' views before speaking, are encouraged to ask why regardless of rank, ask the opinions of others, treat each other with respect, and spend time building trust with each other. Comparatively, all five interviewed participants identified learning and improvement at the individual level since June 18, 2007. Specifically, the CFD is currently more open regarding mistakes, whereas before, the personnel did not take the opportunity to learn from previous errors (P1).

Artifact data provided further indications of learning at the individual level with the retraining of all personnel in the CFD to a higher level, the incorporation of post incident reviews to improve future procedures and responses, a career development plan, enhanced promotional standards, tuition reimbursement, and salary raises for higher education degrees. Further artifact data indicated that the CFD and its personnel are "rising from the ashes of tragedy to become a recognizable symbol of fire service excellence" (Sendelbach, 2012, p. 1). The deputy chief of operations was more effusive in an interview with Foskett (2012), the managing editor of *Fire Rescue Magazine*, where he stated that "the hurdles the members have had to overcome and the processes they have had to learn were extraordinary." He added, "The CFD is an organization filled with extraordinary individuals" (p. 3).

Different views were expressed on the DLOQ (Watkins & Marsick, 1997), interviews, and the artifact data at the team level as well. However, there were specific examples of CFD improvement at this level. Specifically, according to the DLOQ (Watkins & Marsick, 1997) responses, the CFD teams treat members as equals, regardless of rank, culture, or other differences, focus both on the group's task and how well the group is working, and revise their thinking as a result of group discussions or information collected. Comparatively, the interview questions at the team level indicated the utilization of committees by the department now rather than before the June 18, 2007 incident. Specifically, all of the interview participants indicated that before the June 18, 2007 incident, committees were not present, whereas now, they are utilized to help drive the direction of the department (P1, P2, P3, P4, & P5). Furthermore, artifact data indicated that since 2007 the CFD solicited members to organize committees throughout the organization in numerous areas, which has led to the improvement of not only the department operations, but the overall service to the citizens of the community as well (Smith & Elmore, 2013).

Sampled participants also presented different views at the organizational level in the three methods of data. However, results indicated areas organizationally that improved since June 18, 2007. Specifically, according to the DLOQ (Watkins & Marsick, 1997), in the CFD:

- People get needed information at any time quickly and easily.
- An up-to-date database of employee skills is maintained.

- Lessons learned are available to all employees.
- The results of the time and resources spent on training are measured.
- People are recognized for taking initiative.
- People are invited to contribute to the organization's vision.
- People are given control over the resources they need to accomplish their work.
- Alignment of visions is built across different levels and work groups.
- People are encouraged to think from a global perspective.
- Everyone is encouraged to bring the customers' views into the decision-making process.
- The organization works together with the outside community to meet mutual needs.
- People are encouraged to get answers from across the organization when solving problems.
- Leaders generally support requests for learning opportunities and training.
- Leaders share up to date information with employees about competitors, industry trends, and organizational directions.
- Leaders empower others to help carry out the organization's vision.
- Leaders mentor and coach those they lead.
- Leaders continually look for opportunities to learn.
- Leaders ensure that the organization's actions are consistent with its values.

Interview responses focusing on the organizational level indicated that the CFD now focuses more on training, the institution of Critical Incident Reviews to make lessons learned available to the department, and situational assessment. Furthermore, the leadership has changed since June 18, 2007, with all five of the participants acknowledging the effect that the new leadership has had on the organization's development. Moreover, three of the five interview participants indicated that the new leadership has provided the department with beneficial results, and all five participants indicated that leadership training has improved in the organization.

Artifact data was the most effusive at the organizational level, indicating numerous positions created since June 18, 2007, more innovative apparatus purchased, higher levels of training required, better equipment now provided, more advanced procedures developed, the utilization of grants, utilization of community outreach programs, better communication technology instituted, more advanced incident reporting utilized, awards systems were developed, and staffing was increased. Furthermore, Devone-Pacheco (2010) stated that the CFD has made sweeping changes to ensure a similar incident never happens again. Smith and Elmore (2013) added that a recent response to a structure fire in the historic district of Charleston, SC, "demonstrated the fruits of hard lessons learned in the aftermath of the June 2007 Sofa Super Store blaze that killed nine city firefighters" (p. 4).

The aforementioned results from the DLOQ (Watkins & Marsick, 1997), interviews, and artifact data at the individual, team, and organizational levels are significant because they indicated that the CFD learned at all levels following the organizational crisis that ensued following June 18, 2007. These findings compare to James' (2007) study, which indicated that NASA learned following the Challenger disaster and shifted to more of a learning environment, highlighting substantial lessons learned from the organizational crisis. Similarly, Simola's (2005) research regarding Johnson and Johnson's organizational crisis in 1982 indicated that this organization learned significantly following organizational crisis, from the highest level of leadership, to the personnel in charge of operational procedures to combat the crisis. Furthermore, this indicated an improved learning environment that allowed the personnel to improve packaging that had been successful for years and for leaders to eventually increase the company's market sales and shares. This directly relates to the CFD's learning environment since June 18, 2007, and the changes that have been instituted since that tragic day to combat organizational crisis.

Thus, relating to research by Lahteenmaki et al. (2001), a proper response following an incident that leads to an organizational crisis would be for the organization to continuously change and adapt to their operational environment. Overall, the results of this research study indicate the CFD's response following the organizational crisis that ensued post June 18, 2007, and how the organization learned at the individual, team, and organizational levels to continuously change and adapt to their operational environment. Therefore, similar to Simola's (2005) research on Johnson and Johnson's organizational crisis, and James' (2007) study on NASA's crisis, the CFD utilized organizational learning to combat organizational crisis following the loss of nine firefighters on June 18, 2007, in Charleston, SC.

In contrast to the current study's findings, Perkins, et al. (2007) indicated that organizational learning is not a characteristic for transformative change. This presents a difference with the current study on the CFD as results indicated that organizational learning was substantial at the individual, team, and organizational levels following the multiple LODD incident on June 18, 2007, which increased transformative change in the department. Furthermore, Perkins, et al. (2007) indicated that at the individual level, organizations focus on opportunities for task relation, role learning, and personal transformative change. In contrast, the current study on the CFD indicated that at the individual level, continuous learning, inquiry, and dialogue are focused upon by organizations during the transformative process.

CONCLUSION

At the beginning of the data collection, all 21 sampled participants completed Watkins and Marsick's DLOQ (1997) to ascertain how an organization like the CFD learned at the individual, team, and organizational levels following an organizational crisis. According to Davis and Daley (2008), current studies did not outline the possible impact of the individual, team, and organizational elements of an organizations performance, or the assessment approaches to improve upon these elements. Therefore, the significant findings of this study from the DLOQ (Watkins & Marsick, 1997), coupled with the depth of the interviews and artifact data, developed this lacking outline and indicated how the individual, team, and organizational levels impacted an organization's performance.

March and Simon (1958) stated that organizational crises have roots in the external environment. Perrow (1984) expanded upon this research by stating that organizational crises have roots in the malfunctions of an organization. Pearson and Mitroff (1983) and Staw et al. (1981) stated that crises are predominately caused by internal and external factors and can result in catastrophic consequences if the right decisions are not made. A link was presented between the four aforementioned claims and Lin et al. (2006) indicating that the improvement of organizational malfunctions and an increased knowledge of the external environment are essential to the response of accidentally triggered organizational crises that have costly ramifications if not handled correctly. Therefore, these claims may be of value to organizations like the CFD. Thus, this finding is a possible link between the identification of organizational malfunctions and external environment knowledge, and the reduction of the chances of organizational crisis occurring, or in the case that a crisis does occur, to combat it effectively to reduce costly ramifications.

Lahteenmaki et al. (2001) indicated that a proper response following an incident leading to organizational crisis would be for the organization to continuously change and adapt to their operational environment to increase survival and success. This was made possible in the CFD by the recommendations of studies such as *The Routley Report* (2008), completed following the June 18, 2007 incident. Therefore, a link was presented between continuous change and the survival and success of the CFD. Thus, organizations like the CFD may benefit from this finding, as they will be armed to combat the possibility of an organizational crisis with the knowledge that continuous change and adaptation to their external environment will increase organizational survival and success.

Jasko et al. (2012) posited that the value of knowing how to learn is critical to increasing the survivability of future crisis. James (2007) indicated that NASA utilized learning in their response following the Challenger disaster, improving their response to a future disaster of similar magnitude, the Columbia disaster. The learning that took place during this time period increased the survivability of the organization following the future crisis. There is link between NASA's response to their disasters and the CFD's response to its disaster on June 18, 2007. This finding offers the possibility that due to the CFD knowing how to learn as indicated by the study's results, their response to a future crisis would be similar to NASA's improved response. Therefore, it is possible that since the CFD understands the value of knowing how to learn, they are better equipped to respond to organizational crisis in a more effective manner, increasing organizational survival and success.

Brong (2004) posited, "Learning from the accident that claimed the Columbia and its crew is an extraordinary responsibility" (p. 39). Comparatively, it is an extraordinary responsibility for the CFD to learn from the incident on June 18, 2007. This presents a significant commonality between James (2007) and this research study. Therefore, a possible link is presented between organizations experiencing organizational crisis and their responsibility to learn from the crisis to ensure that they, as well as other organizations, benefit from this grave period of time.

The research findings converge to answer the study's research questions. The findings show that the CFD has successfully recovered from the grave consequences of organizational crisis. Furthermore, the research and investigation surrounding the study has advanced the scientific knowledge in this area and has filled a gap in the research regarding how an organization like the CFD learned following organizational crisis at the individual, team, and organizational levels.

IMPLICATIONS

The theoretical orientation of this study involved researching organizational crisis through the lens of organizational learning. The data collected and analyzed for this study were attained from the participants and artifact data on the subject. The participant's data sources, the DLOQ (Watkins & Marsick, 1997) and the interviews, were presented in their words, with the artifact data presented exactly from the sources or in a paraphrased manner. An area of strength of the study was reflected in the fact that sampled participants all officially responded to June 18, 2007, and were still employed with the CFD at the time of this study. This allowed them to view the organization at the individual, team, and organizational levels before this tragic day, to the present state of the organization. A second strength of the study was presented with 21 out of the 27 possible participants who officially responded to the event on June 18, 2007, according to Firehouse reporting, and were still employed at the time of the study participating.

A weakness of the study included the fact that only firefighters from the CFD were studied. Other agencies also responded to the event on June 18, 2007. Therefore, future studies are needed to incorporate the other responding agencies to ascertain if they experienced an organizational crisis and, if so, did they utilize organizational learning to improve upon the crisis. This would add to the body of knowledge of organizational crisis and organizational learning further.

Another weakness of the study included the fact that the researcher was the interviewer during the data collection process. After conducting the study, the researcher identified that future case studies are needed involving interviews conducted by an outside individual, rather than the researcher. However, with the execution of the study by the researcher, 100% anonymity was ensured and established, particularly relative to the high degree of sensitivity of the subject under discussion. The completion of a study with an individual to administer the interviews other than the researcher would ensure that the perception of coercion was reduced and that a purposeful conversation regarding the participants' experience could be attained (Kvale & Brinkman, 2008).

The literature review of the study, Chapter 2, was the foundation for this research. Gaps in the literature included understanding how an organization like the CFD learned from an organizational crisis at the individual, team, and organizational levels. After a thorough examination of the literature, the study design emerged.

The review of the literature found that organizational learning is divided into two distinct theories: single loop learning and double loop learning (Argyris, 2002). Single loop learning is defined as correcting errors without changing underlying governing values, whereas double loop learning implies the correction of errors by altering the governing values and actions (Argyris, 2002). Relative to this consideration, Yang et al. (2004) posited that organizational learning and the learning organization are "two related yet distinct constructs" that have their differences (p. 34).

The learning organization construct usually pertains to organizations that display continuous learning and adaptive characteristics, or those who are attempting to institute them. In contrast, organizational learning identifies collective learning experiences utilized to develop skills and attain knowledge (Yang et al., 2004). It can be argued that in order to institute and display continuous learning and adaptive characteristics, collective learning experiences must be first identified to attain the knowledge and skills to do so.

The study was grounded in the organizational learning theory as it allowed for the identification, measurement, and description of how an organization like the CFD learned from an organizational crisis following June 18, 2007 at the individual, team, and organizational levels. Previous studies were completed on organizational learning with qualitative models in for-profit organizations, as well as NASA (James, 2007; Yeo, 2007). The settings for these studies included NASA in James (2007) and a large manufacturing firm in Singapore in Yeo (2007). James (2007) focused on how NASA learned following the Columbia and Challenger incidents, and Yeo (2007) focused on factors that were indicative of organizational learning and effectiveness. From the literature review, it was discovered that "learning from the accident that claimed the Columbia and its crew is an extraordinary responsibility" (Brong, 2004, p. 39). Therefore, it is an extraordinary responsibility of the CFD to learn from the incident that claimed nine firefighters and pass on the lessons learned to other organizations.

The review of the literature also indicated that an organizational crisis reveals organizational management's capability to handle this type of event (Coldwell et al., 2012). During this critical time in an organization, effective strategies and resources utilized to handle the situation efficiently must be ensured to minimize damaging exposure to the media and organizational stakeholders. However, if the crisis is handled successfully, the organization may enhance their products, services, and reputation (Coldwell et al., 2012; Senge, 1990). When this occurs, organizational learning has been utilized in order to progress from a negative event to a positive learning environment that focuses on the enhancement of products or services from lessons witnessed from previous occurrences.

Strategic leadership is also important following these types of negative events for learning, empowerment of the personnel toward a collective vision, the creation of systems to capture and share learning, to encourage collaboration and team learning, to promote inquiry and dialogue, to create continuous learning opportunities, and to transform the organization so that it can prevent or improve responses to future crisis (Watkins & Marsick, 1997). Other learning theories that can be utilized to respond to organizational crisis include Kolb's (1984) experiential learning theory (ELT), which focuses on physiology, psychology, and philosophy, Senge's (1990) adaptive and generative learning theory, which utilizes mental models as an integral component, and the Nevis et al. (1995) assimilation theory that incorporates three unique stages in the learning process. These stages include knowledge acquisition, knowledge sharing, and knowledge utilization (Leavitt, 2011).

THEORETICAL IMPLICATIONS

As of the publication date of this study, there was little integration between organizational crisis and organizational change (Maitlis & Sonenshein, 2010). Specifically, a gap in the literature was presented relative to organizational crisis and organizational learning following this type of crisis. Therefore, introducing the effects of organizational crisis and the importance of organizational learning to combat or prevent this type of crisis in organizations like the CFD, can lead to safer, more efficient practices, and may save the lives of firefighters.

This theoretical implication involves the ability of organizations like the CFD to utilize organizational learning in response to organizational crisis, which is considered extraordinary, damaging, and disruptive to an organization's state of operations (Snyder et al., 2006). This implication supports research by Senge (1990), indicating that organizations can become learning organizations and that through the learning of individual members, organizations can change. In further support of this implication, research indicated evidence had been found that can help organizations recover and grow from the grave consequences of an organizational crisis with organizational learning. This was exhibited in James' (2007) study on NASA's organizational crisis, indicating that the organization learned from their previous lack of transparency following the Challenger disaster. This allowed them to combat future organizational crisis following the Columbia disaster.

PRACTICAL IMPLICATIONS

The practical implication of this study is its ability to educate leaders on the consequences of organizational crisis, and in turn, guide them to utilize organizational learning to combat this type of crisis or to prevent it altogether. Lack of literature relative to organizational crisis and organizational learning following this type of tragedy presents a gap in the literature. However, organizations can utilize the research presented in this study to their advantage because now organizations like the CFD know what organizational crisis looks like and have a better understanding of how organizational learning plays an important role in responding to the crisis. Additionally, this study can be utilized as an advantage to other organizations, even if they have not experienced an organizational crisis. This research will allow them to identify areas in their respective organization where they may be lacking, and in turn, implement the needed changes to prevent organizational crisis from occurring with the use of organizational learning.

The questionnaire utilized by the 21 sampled participants was independently completed, as were the five randomly selected interviews. The design allowed all participants to voice their perceptions of the CFD at the individual, team, and organizational levels. None of the participants were educated on the two theories focused upon in this study. The findings of this study indicated that the CFD learned following organizational crisis at the individual, team, and organizational levels. However, there is still work to be done is some areas.

FUTURE IMPLICATIONS

The future implications connected to this study are based on what the qualitative case study did find and what the study did not find. Results of the study revealed that the CFD learned from organizational crisis at the individual, team, and organizational levels. Thus, other organizations that experience this type of crisis should consider utilizing organizational learning to combat the grave consequences of organizational crisis or to identify areas that are lacking in their organization and improve upon them to reduce the chances of an organizational crisis. The experiences of the sampled participants were theirs alone. However, it was assumed that other firefighters from the CFD that responded to the event on June 18, 2007, and are still employed with the CFD, experienced the organizational crisis in a similar way, based upon the fact that they were present during the event and are still employed with the CFD, as of the date of this publication.

This study did not include a longitudinal view of how the CFD's learning continued to improve or persist at the individual, team, and organizational levels. Thus, follow-ups with sampled participants would identify if the CFD continued to learn following organizational crisis at the individual, team, and organizational levels. Furthermore, the research study did not include CFD responders that unofficially responded to the event on June 18, 2007, and were still employed with the CFD. Changing the sample to responders that unofficially responded and were still employed with the CFD encourages the development of comparative studies to identify if there are connections between the two groups of responders' perception of the organizational crisis and organizational learning following June 18, 2007. This study's methodology can also incorporate a different setting with the replacement of a fire service organization with a law enforcement organization. Law enforcement agencies respond to rapidly unfolding events that pose life threatening situations and unexpected risks also; therefore, this research methodology needs to be replicated in a law enforcement agency as well (Baran & Scott, 2010). The sampled participants of this research study did not relate organizational learning to improvement upon organizational crisis. However, this is because the sampled participants had never experienced an organizational crisis of this magnitude, or utilized organizational learning to prevent or combat this type of crisis. Understanding the future implications of this research study enables the researcher to present recommendations for future research and practice.

RECOMMENDATIONS

Included in this final section of the research study's findings and conclusions are recommendations for future research and practices related to the studied constructs. These recommendations include four possible qualitative research studies to increase the understanding of the importance of the use of organizational learning to prevent or combat organizational crisis. Included in each recommendation for future research is suggested methodology and design. Future practice recommendations include two suggestions for implementing organizational learning into all organizations, not only those oriented toward emergency services.

RECOMMENDATIONS FOR FUTURE RESEARCH

The literature review that grounded this study in theory indicated a lack of research regarding the use of organizational learning in organizations to combat organizational crisis. The sampled participants utilized in this study officially responded to the event of June 18, 2007 and were still employed with the CFD at the time of the study, according to Firehouse reporting. Thus, firefighters that responded to the event unofficially and were still employed with the CFD at the time of this research were not studied. Therefore, a future recommendation for research includes completing this qualitative case study with firefighters that unofficially responded to the June 18, 2007 event, and were still employed with the CFD, to explore how they were affected by the organizational crisis that ensued, and the role organizational learning played to combat the crisis.

Another recommendation for research would include the study of the multiple agencies that responded to the event on June 18, 2007, and how they responded to the organizational crisis in their respective organizations with the use of organizational learning. The study would be similar in nature to this study in that it would incorporate a qualitative methodology and case study design. The research would utilize questionnaires, interviews, and surveys with personnel from all rank levels focused upon to construct a converging line of inquiry.

The third recommendation for future research includes a study of a law enforcement agency that has experienced a line of duty death (LODD), leading to an organizational crisis. A qualitative case study would be utilized in this study as well, incorporating questionnaires, surveys, and interviews. The focus of the study would be on the leadership of the organization to gain perceptions of how this type of event encourages changes on the leadership front with the use of organizational learning. The purpose of this study would be to understand specifically how leaders respond during times of crisis, differing from the current study which focused on all personnel levels of an organization.

The final recommendation for future research includes the study of a military organization that has experienced numerous events that have led to LODD's. Specifically, how they utilized organizational learning to respond to these events would be considered. The study would utilize a qualitative methodology and case study design focused on the soldiers that were involved in the events where their fellow soldiers perished, rather than the leadership. This study would include the use of interviews, questionnaires, and artifact data.

RECOMMENDATIONS FOR PRACTICE

The results of this study indicate the positive effects that organizational learning has on recovering from the grave consequences of organizational crisis. No unrelated or speculative information unsupported by data was presented. Each participant was understanding about the relevance of the study and intrigued to participate in work that could save lives. Therefore, the first recommendation for practice based on findings from this study incorporates the development and institution of organizational crisis and organizational learning curriculum into not only emergency service organizations, but all types of organizations as well. Knowledge of the consequences that result in an organizational crisis and how organizational learning can be utilized to prevent and combat this type of crisis may improve operations, leadership, technology, and equipment used in all types of organizations.

Secondly and finally, it is recommended that organizational learning be practiced in all types of organizations. According to Elliot (2009), the continuing failure of organizations to learn from organizational crisis creates political, social, financial, and individual costs that are attributable to the misunderstanding of learning processes. Therefore, this recommendation is given with the expectation that a change can be made in the arena of organizational learning and that this theory will be used not only in times of crisis, but in times of preparation and organizational improvement.

EPILOGUE

So, why are these results important? Captain Mike Benke, Captain Billy Hutchinson, Captain Louis Mulkey, Engineer Mark Kelsey, Engineer Brad Baity, Assistant Engineer Michael French, Firefighter Earl Drayton, Firefighter Brandon Thompson, Firefighter Melvin Champaign, and all of the firefighters who gave the ultimate sacrifice. If we do not learn from the events that led to their deaths, we are not honoring their memory or fulfilling our obligation to NEVER FORGET.

In order to fulfill this obligation, we must continue to change to keep up with the advancement of technology in our operational environment. Is this hard at times? Yes. It's hard for everyone. But we must put our best foot forward and march on. Negativity breeds negativity and nothing good comes out of that. If we would focus our energies every day to make one positive change that we were struggling with, we would grow continually. It's all in our attitude. I fought it every step of the way at first, and all it did was make me miserable and others around me feel the same way. This is counterproductive to advancement, and tramples on the hearts of the fallen.

The results of this study prove the progress that has been made by the CFD since that tragic day in 2007. Are we perfect? Definitely not. No one or no organization is. However, we are continually learning to ensure we provide our people with the right equipment, the right training, and the right tactics that they need to succeed. It has been a long, hard fight, and will continue to be that way until we reach excellence. No one ever said it would be easy. We have made it this far, so strap on your grown up pants and it's go time. We can't live in the past, when the present rate of technology and innovation is changing faster now than any time in history.

Every organization that I am blessed to travel to and speak with regarding my research, people ask me how I dug myself out of the hole I was in and why did I stay. Well first, I have the amazing support of my family, as well as the people that I work with. Even during the times of my anger, my alcohol and prescription drug abuse, my wild lifestyle, and my want to fight anyone that looked my way, my family, friends, and firefighting family didn't turn their back on me. They could have chalked me up to a lost soul, but they didn't. I thank the big man upstairs for that every day and now I realize how truly blessed I am. Sometimes you have to take a wrong turn to find the right road. It's part of life.

Okay, now the tough one. Why did I stay? My answer to them is simple. How could I leave and why would I? I cannot and will not walk away from those nine men that lost their lives on June 18, 2007. I will continue to change and honor them in every aspect of my life. One day if the Good Lord allows me to reach the Pearly Gates, my nine friends will be standing there and they will ask me what I did to honor their sacrifice and make sure the fire service learned and changed from that catastrophic event. I am comfortable with my answer. Yes, I still feel the pain every day. Yes, I still cry about it. Yes, I still lose sleep. Yes, I still have flashbacks. Yes, I still want to go drink my pain away. But I DO NOT. I will not give in to the pain and sadness. I march on for change to ensure this type of tragedy does not happen again.

In closing, according to Karl Paul Reinhold Niebuhr, American theologian and the recipient of the 1964 Presidential Medal of Freedom, "Change is the essence of life. Be willing to surrender what you are, for what you could become." **Are you willing to surrender what you are, for what you could become?** Give it a chance and you could become something magnificent. This attitude will permeate through an organization if one person will just stand up and start the mission for change and progressiveness. It's in your hands. If you don't do it, you have no one to blame but yourself. The MISSION is calling . . . answer the call and change not only your organization, but your life as well.

REFERENCES

Accenture. (2011). *Corporate crisis management.* Retrieved from http://www.accenture.com/

Anthony, D. (1994). Managing the disaster. *Fire Engineering, 147*(8), 22-40. Retrieved from http://www.fireengineering.com/index.html

Argyris, C. (1990). *Overcoming organizational defenses: Facilitating organizational learning.* Englewood Cliffs, NJ: Prentice Hall.

Argyris, C. (1982). The executive mind and double-loop learning. *Organizational Dynamics, 11*(2), 5-22. Retrieved from http://www.abielg.com/filestoprobal/92-the%20executive%20 mind%20and%20the%20double%20loop%20learning.pdf

Argyris, C. (2002). Double-loop learning, teaching, and research. *Academy of Management Learning & Education, 1*(2), 206-218. doi:10.5465/AMLE.2002.8509400

Aslam, H., Javaid, T., Tanveer, A., Khan, M., & Shabbir, F. (2011). A journey from individual to organizational learning. (Exploring the linking bridge: Team learning). *International Journal of Academic Research, 3*(3), 738-745. Retrieved from http://www.ijar.lit.az/

Baran, B. E., & Scott, C. W. (2010). Organizing ambiguity: A grounded theory of leadership and sense making within dangerous contexts. *Military Psychology, 22*(1), 2242-2269. doi:10.1080/08995601003644262

Baxter, P., & Jack, S. (2008). Qualitative case study methodology:

Study design and implementation for novice researchers. *The Qualitative Report, 13*(4), 544-559. Retrieved
from http://www.nova.edu/ssss/QR/QR13-4/baxter.pdf

Bea, B. (2006). Learning from failures: Lessons from the recent history of failures of engineered systems. *Center for Catastrophic
Risk Management. University of California, Berkley.* Retrieved
from http://ccrm.berkeley.edu/pdfs_papers/bea_pdfs/learning
_from_failures2.pdf

Berthoin-Antal, A., Lenhardt, U., & Rosenbrock, R. (2003). Barriers
to organizational learning. In M. Dierks, A. B. Berthoin-Antal, J.
Child, and I. Nonaka (Eds.), *Handbook of organizational learning and knowledge* (pp. 865-885). Oxford: Oxford University
Press.

Bischoff, G. (2010). The firefighter's firefighter. *Fire Chief Magazine.*
Retrieved from http://firechief.com/leadership/ar/tom-carr-
career-coy-201009

Boatright, J. R. (2000). *Ethics and the conduct of business* (3rd ed.).
Upper Saddle River, NJ: Prentice Hall.

Brookfield, S. D. (2000). Transformative learning as ideology critique. In J. Mezirow and Associates (Eds.), *Learning as transformation: Critical perspectives on a theory in progress* (pp. 125-148).
San Francisco, CA: Jossey-Bass.

Brong, J. (2004). Learning from Columbia. *Quality Progress, 37*(3),
38-45. Retrieved from http://asq.org/quality-press/journal/
index.html?item=SUBSCR_QP

Carr, L. T. (1994). The strengths and weaknesses of quantitative and qualitative research: What method for nursing? *Journal of Advanced Nursing, 20*(4), 716-721.

doi:10.1046/j.1365-2648.1994.20040716.x

Carroll, G. R., & Hannan, M. T. (2000). *The demography of corporations and industries*. Princeton, NJ: Princeton University Press.

Caywood, C., & Stocker, K. P. (1993). The ultimate crisis plan. In J. Gottschalk (Ed.), *Crisis response: Inside stories on managing image under siege* (pp. 409-428). Washington, DC: Gale Research.

Charleston Fire Department. (2009). Memo 09-13. Improved communications–Email, 1. Charleston, SC.

Charleston Fire Department. (2009). Memo 09-7. John Tippett, 1. Charleston, SC.

Charleston Fire Department. (2009). Memo Tuition Reimbursement, 1. Charleston, SC.

Charleston Fire Department. (2009). Memo Career Development, 1. Charleston, SC.

Charleston Fire Department. (2009). Memo Promotional Exam Writers, 1. Charleston, SC.

Charleston Fire Department. (2009). Memo Promotional Exam Development Teams, 1. Charleston, SC.

Charleston Fire Department. (2011). Memo 11-9, Firehouse Narrative, 1. Charleston, SC.

Charleston Fire Department. (2012). Memo 12-04, Personal Grooming, 1 - 2. Charleston, SC.

Charleston Fire Department. (2013). Memo 13-08. Emergency Response Modifications–Local Alarms, 1. Charleston, SC.

Charleston Fire Department. (2013). Memo 13-09. Leave Changes Due to Budget, 1. Charleston, SC.

Charleston Fire Department. (2013). Memo 13-15. Assistant Engineer Requirements - Interim, 1 - 2. Charleston, SC.

Charleston Fire Department. (2009). Standard Operating Procedure 201.07 Post Incident Review, 1. Charleston, SC.

Charleston Fire Department. (2009). Standard Operating Procedure 201.07a Post Incident Review Form, 1-3. Charleston, SC.

Charleston Fire Department. (2009). Standard Operating Procedure 115.08 Transfer Policy, 1. Charleston, SC.

Charleston Fire Department. (2011). Standard Operating Procedure 115.01 Shift Scheduling and Electronic Roster, 1-4. Charleston, SC.

Charleston Fire Department. (2011). Standard Operating Procedure 606.04 After the Fire Neighborhood Canvas, 1-4. Charleston, SC.

Charleston Fire Department. (2012). Standard Operating Procedure 200.01 Safe Structural Firefighting, 1-59. Charleston, SC.

Charleston Fire Department. (2013). Standard Operating Procedure 101.2 Promotion to Engineer, 1. Charleston, SC.

Charleston Fire Department. (2013). Standard Operating Procedure 101.3 Promotion to Captain. Charleston, SC.

Charleston Fire Department. (2013). Standard Operating Procedure 101.4 Promotion to Battalion Chief, 1 - 2. Charleston, SC.

Charleston Fire Department. (2013). Standard Operating Procedure 102.1 Code of Conduct and General Orders, 1-7. Charleston, SC.

Charleston Fire Department. (2013). Standard Operating Procedure 116.01 Awards Program, 1 - 7. Charleston, SC.

Charleston Fire Department. (2013). Strategic Plan 2013–2015, 41. Charleston Fire Department Strategic Planning Committee, Charleston SC.

Clark, L. (1999). *Mission improbable: Using fantasy documents to tame disaster.* Chicago, IL: The University of Chicago Press.

Coldwell, D., Joosub, T., & Papageorgiou, E. (2012). Responsible leadership in organizational crises: An analysis of the effects of public perceptions of selected SA business organizations' reputations. *Journal of Business Ethics, 109*(2), 133-144. doi:10.1007/s10551-011-1110-8

Collins, J. C., & Porras, J. I. (2000). *Built to last: Successful habits of visionary companies* (3rd ed.). London: Random House Business Books.

Cooke, D. (1994). L.A. earthquake puts city disaster planning to test. *Disaster Recovery Journal, 7*(4), 10-12. Retrieved from http://www.drj.com/drj-world-archives/earthquakes/la-earthquake-puts-city-disaster-planning-to-test.html

Crisis. (n.d.). In *Merriam Webster online.* Retrieved from http://www.merriam-webster.com/

Cummings, T. G., & Worley, C. G. (1997). *Organizational development and change.* Cincinnati, OH: South-Western College Publishing.

Daft, R. L. (1999). *Leadership theory and practice.* Fort Worth, TX: The Dryden Press.

Davis, D. (2005). The learning organization and its dimensions as key factors in firm performance. *Dissertation Abstracts International.* (UMI No. 3168204). doi:10.1080/13678860701782352

Davis, D., & Daley, B. J. (2008). The learning organization and its dimensions as key factors in firms' performance. *Human Resource Development International, 11*(1), 51-66. doi:10.1080/13678860701782352

Denton, N. (1998). *Organizational learning and effectiveness.* London:

Routledge.

Devone-Pacheco, C. (2010). Then & now: The truth about Charleston from the last officer out. Retrieved from http://my.firefighternation.com/profiles/blogs/then-amp-now-the-truth-about

Devone-Pacheco, C. (2012). Charleston five years later: An officer's perspective. *Fire Fighter Nation*. Retrieved from http://www.firefighternation.com/article/command-and-leadership/charleston-five-years-later-officer-s-perspective

Dodgson, M. (1993). Organizational learning: A review of some literatures. *Organizational Studies, 14*(3), 375-394. doi:10.1177/017084069301400303

Duffy, M. E. (1985). Designing nursing research: The qualitative–quantitative debate. *Journal of Advanced Nursing, 10*(3), 225-232. doi:10.1111/j.1365-2648.1985.tb00516.x

Dutton, J. E., & Jackson S. E. (1987). Categorizing strategic issues: Links to organizational action. *Academy of Management Review, 12*(1), 76-90. doi:10.5465/AMR.1987.4306483

Dynes, R. (1970). *Organized behavior in disaster*. Lexington, MA: Heath.

Egan, T., Yang, B., & Barlett, K. R. (2004). The effects of organizational learning culture and job satisfaction on motivation to transfer learning and turnover intention. *Human Resource Development Quarterly, 15*(3), 279-301. doi:10.1002/hrdq.1104

Elliott, D. (2009). The failure of organizational learning from crisis–A matter of life and death? *Journal of Contingencies & Crisis Management, 17*(3), 157-168. doi:10.1111/j.1468-5973.2009.00576.x

Ellinger, A. D., Ellinger, A. E., Yang, B., & Howton, S. W. (2002).

The relationship between the learning organization concept and firms' financial performance: An empirical assessment. *Human Resource Development Quarterly, 13*(1), 5-21. doi:10.1002/hrdq.1010

Farazmand, A. (2007). Learning from the Katrina crisis: A global and international perspective with implications for future crisis management. *Public Administration Review, 67*(S1), 149-159. doi:10.1111/j.1540-6210.2007.00824.x

Feagin, J., Orum, A., & Sjoberg, G. (Eds.). (1991). *A case for case study.* Chapel Hill, NC: University of North Carolina Press.

Fink, S. (1986). *Crisis management: Planning for the inevitable.* New York, NY: American Management Association.

Firehouse Reporting. (2013). *The City of Charleston Fire Department (CFD).* Retrieved from Firehouse online registered to the CFD.

Fombrun, J. C., & Van Riel, C. B. M. (2004). *Fame and fortune: How successful companies build winning reputations.* Upper Saddle River, NJ: Prentice Hall.

Foskett, J. (2012a). Tippett: Critics wouldn't recognize the CFD. *Fire Fighter Nation.* Retrieved from http://www.firefighternation.com/article/command-and-leadership/tippett-critics-wouldn-t-recognize-cfd

Foskett, J. (2012b). Investigation team leader sees significant improvements at CFD. *Fire Fighter Nation.* Retrieved from http://www.firefighternation.com/article/command-and-leadership/investigation-team-leader-sees-significant-improvements-cfd

Garvin, D. A., Edmondson, A. C., & Gino, F. (2008). Is yours a learning organization? *Harvard Business Review, 86*(3), 109. Retrieved from http://hbr.org/2008/03/is-yours-a-learning-organization/

ar/1

Gau, W., & Wen, C. (2011). Insurance agencies' organizational learning in a turbulent time: A community of practice perspective. *Journal of Modern Education Review, 1*(1), 41-49. Retrieved from http://academicstar.ecrater.com/p/11598874/journal-of-modern-education-review

Gephart, R. (2007). Crisis sense making and the public inquiry. In C. M. Pearson, C. Roux-Dufort, and J. Clair (Eds.), *An international handbook of organizational crisis management.* Thousand Oaks, CA: Sage Publications.

Gibbs, G. (2007). *Analyzing qualitative data.* London: Sage Publications.

Gledhill, S., Abbey, J., & Schweitzer, R. (2008). Sampling methods: Methodological issues involved in the recruitment of older people into a study of sexuality. *Australian Journal of Advanced Nursing, 26*(1), 84-94. Retrieved from http://eprints.qut.edu.au/15009/1/15009.pdf

Goh, S. C. (1998). Toward a learning organization: The strategic building blocks. *S.A.M. Advanced Management Journal, 63*(2), 15-20. Retrieved from http://retention-research.wikispaces.com/file/view/Toward+a+learning+organization_The+strategic+building+blocks_Goh.pdf

Hatch, J. A. (2002). *Doing qualitative research in education settings.* Albany, NY: State University of New York Press.

Hernandez, M. (2000). *The impact of the dimensions of the learning organization on the transfer of tacit knowledge process and performance improvement within private manufacturing firms in Colombia.* (Unpublished Ph.D. thesis). University of Georgia,

Athens.

Hsu, G., & Hannan M. T. (2005). Identities, genres, and organizational forms. *Organization Science, 16*(5), 474–490. doi:10.1287/orsc.1050.0151

Ioannidis, J. (2007). Limitations are not properly acknowledged in the scientific literature. *Journal of Clinical Epidemiology, 60*(4), 324-329. doi:10.1016/j.jclinepi.2006.09.011

Illeris, K. (2007). *How we learn: Learning and non-learning in school and beyond.* London, England: Routledge.

Irving, P. G., Coleman, D. F., & Cooper, C. L. (1997). Further assessments of a three-component model of occupational commitment: Generalizability and differences across occupations. *Journal of Applied Psychology, 82*(3), 444-452. doi:10.1037//0021-9010.82.3.444

Jacob, S. A., & Furgerson, S. (2012). Writing interview protocols and conducting interviews: Tips for students new to the field of qualitative research. *Qualitative Report, 17.* Retrieved from http://www.nova.edu/ssss/QR/QR17/jacob.pdf

James, E. (2007). A case study of NASA's Columbia tragedy: An organizational learning and sense making approach to organizational crisis. (M.A. dissertation). University of North Texas, Texas.

James, X., Hawkins, A., & Rowel, R. (2007). An assessment of the cultural appropriateness of emergency preparedness communication for low-income minorities. *Journal of Homeland Security and Emergency Management, 4*(3), 1-24. doi:10.2202/1547-7355.1266

Jasko, O., Popovic, N., & Prokic, S. (2012). The importance of knowledge management for the improvement of crisis management. *China-USA Business Review, 11*(2), 268-274. Retrieved from http://www.chinabusinessreview.com/

Jones, S., Murphy, F., Edwards, M., & James. (2008). Doing things differently: Advantages and disadvantages of web questionnaires. *Nurse Researcher, 15*(4), 15-26. Retrieved from http://nurseresearcher.rcnpublishing.co.uk/archive/article-doing-things-differently-advantages-and-disadvantages-of-web-questionnaires

Kelley, K., Clark, B., Vivienne, B., & Sitzia, J. (2003). Good practice in the conduct and reporting of survey research. *International Journal for Quality in Health Care, 15*(3), 261-266. doi:10.1093/intqhc/mzg031

Klann, G. (2003). *Crisis leadership.* Greensboro, NC: Center for Leadership Press.

Knafl, K., & Breitmayer, B. J. (1989). Triangulation in qualitative research: Issues of conceptual clarity and purpose. In J. M. Morse (Ed.), *Qualitative nursing research: A contemporary dialogue* (pp. 193-203). Rockville, MD: Aspen.

Kolb, D. (1984). *Experiential learning: Experience as the source of learning and development.* Upper Saddle River, NJ: Prentice Hall.

Kreber, C. (2005). Reflection on teaching and epistemological structure: Reflective and critically reflective processes in 'pure/soft' and 'pure/hard' fields. *Higher Education, 57*(4), 509-531. doi:10.1007/s10734-008-9158-9

Kroeber, A. L., & Kluckhohn, C. (1952). *Culture: A critical review of concepts and definitions.* New York, NY: Vintage Books.

Kvale, S., & Brinkman, S. (2008). *Interviews: Learning the craft of qualitative research interviewing.* Thousand Oaks, CA: Sage

Publications.

Lähteenmäki, S., Toivonen, J., & Mattila, M. (2001). Critical aspects of organizational learning research and proposals for its measurement. *British Journal of Management, 12*(2), 113-129. doi:10.1111/1467-8551.00189

Larson, R., Bengtsson, L., Henriksson, K., & Sparks, J. (1998). The interorganizational learning dilemma: Collective knowledge development in strategic alliances. *Organization Science, 9*(3), 285-286. doi:10.1287/orsc.9.3.285

Leach, M. (1990). Philosophical choice: Nursing. *The Journal of Clinical Practice, Education and Management, 4*(3), 16-18. Retrieved from http://journalseek.net/cgi-bin/journalseek/journalsearch.cgi?field=issn&query=0142-0372

Leavitt, C. C. (2011). A comparative analysis of three unique theories of organizational learning. Retrieved from ERIC database. (ED523990)

Lee, A. S., & Baskerville, R. L. (2012). Conceptualizing generalizability: New contributions and a reply. *MIS Quarterly, 36*(3), 749-A7. Retrieved from http://www.misq.org/skin/frontend/default/misq/pdf/appendices/2012/V36I3_Appendices/LeeBaskervilleAppendices.pdf

Lengnick-Hall, C., & Beck, T. (2003). *Beyond bouncing back: The concept of organizational resilience.* Seattle, WA: The Academy of Management.

Lien, B. Y., Hung, R. Y., Yang, B., & Li, M. (2006). Is the learning organization a valid concept in the Taiwanese context? *International Journal of Manpower, 27*(2), 189-203. doi:10.1108/01437720610666209

Lin, Z., Xia, Z., Ismail, K. M., & Carley, K. M. (2006). Organizational design and restructuring in response to crises: Lessons from computational modeling and real-world cases. *Organization Science, 17*(5), 598-618. doi:10.1287/orsc.1060.0210

López, S. P., Montes Peón, J. M., & Ordás, C. J. V. (2006). Human resources management as a determining factor in organizational learning. *Management Learning, 37*(2), 215-239. doi:10.1177/1350507606063443

Lynn, G., Simpson J., & Souder, W. (1997). Effects of organizational learning and information-processing behaviors on new product success. *Marketing Letters, 8*(1), 33-39. doi:10.1023/A:1007981109972

Maak, T., & Pless, N. (2006). *Responsible leadership.* New York, NY: Routledge.

Maitlis, S., & Sonenshein, S. (2010). Sense making in crisis and change: Inspiration and insights from Weick (1988). *Journal of Management Studies, 47*(3), 551-580. doi:10.1111/j.1467-6486.2010.00908.x

Malkki, K. (2012). Rethinking disorienting dilemmas within real-life crises: The role of reflection in negotiating emotionally chaotic experiences. *Adult Education Quarterly, 62*(3), 207-229. doi:10.1177/0741713611402047

Mallak, L. (1998). *Resilience in the Healthcare Industry. Industrial Engineering Research Conference.* Albert, Canada: Banff.

March, J. G., & Simon, H. A. (1958). *Organizations.* New York, NY: John Wiley & Sons.

Marrelli, A. F. (2007). Collecting data through case studies. *Performance Improvement, 46*(7), 39-44. doi:10.1002/pfi.148

Marsick, V., & Watkins, K. (2003). Demonstrating the value of an organization's learning culture: The dimensions of the learning organization questionnaire. *Advances in Developing Human Resources, 5*(2), 132-151. doi:10.1177/1523422303005002002

Martin, A., & Brun, R. (2009). Proceedings from I-KNOW '09 and I-SEMANTICS '09. Graz, Austria. Retrieved from http://mature-ip.eu/files/papers/iknow09/applying_organizational_learning.pdf

McHargue, S. K. (1999). *Dimensions of the learning organization as determinants of organizational performance in nonprofit organizations.* Athens, GA: University of Georgia.

Mezirow, J. (2009). An overview of transformative learning. In K. Illeris (Ed.), *Contemporary theories of learning...Learning theorists in their own words* (pp. 90-105). London, England: Routledge.

Moon, J. (2004). *A handbook of reflective and experiential learning: Theory and practice.* London: Routledge Falmer.

National Institute of Standards and Technology. (2012). *U.S. Department of Commerce.* Retrieved from http://www.nist.gov/index.html

Nevis, E. C., DiBella, A. J., & Gould, J. M. (1995). Understanding organizations as learning systems. *MIT Sloan Management Review, 36*(2), 73. Retrieved from http://sloanreview.mit.edu/article/understanding-organizations-as-learning-systems/

Nisbet, J., & Watt, J. (1984). *Conducting small-scale investigations in educational management* (pp. 79-92). London: Harper & Row.

Occupational Safety and Health Administration. (2012). *United States Department of Labor.* Retrieved from http://www.osha.

gov/

Olofsson, A. (2007). Crisis communication in multicultural societies: A study of municipalities in Sweden. *International Journal of Mass Emergencies and Disasters, 25*(2), 145-172. Retrieved from http://ijmed.org/

Olofsson, A. (2011). Organizational crisis preparedness in heterogeneous societies: The OCPH model. *Journal of Contingencies and Crisis Management, 19*(4), 215-226. doi:10.1111/j.1468-5973.2011.00652.x

Organization. (n.d.). In *Merriam Webster online.* Retrieved from http://www.merriam-webster.com/

Ortenbald, A. (2004). The learning organization: Towards an integrated model. *The Learning Organization, 11*(2/3), 129-144. doi:10.1108/09696470410521592

Paine, L. P. (1994). Managing for organizational integrity. *Harvard Business Review, 72*(2), 106-117. Retrieved from http://hbr.org/1994/03/managing-for-organizational-integrity/ar/1

Palmerino, M. B. (1999). Take a quality approach to qualitative research. *Marketing News, 33*(12), 35. Retrieved from http://www.marketingpower.com/AboutAMA/Pages/AMA%20Publications/Marketing%20News/MarketingNews.aspx

Pearson, C. M., & Mitroff, C. M. (1983). *Crisis management: A diagnostic guide for improving your organizations' crisis preparedness.* San Francisco, CA: Jossey-Bass Publishers.

Pedler, M., Burgoyne, J., & Boydell, T. (1991). *The learning company: A strategy for sustainable development.* London: McGraw-Hill.

Perkins, D. D., Bess, K. D., Cooper, D. G., Jones, D. L., Armstead, T., & Speer, P. W. (2007). Community organizational learning:

Case studies illustrating a three-dimensional model of levels and orders of change. *Journal of Community Psychology, 35*(3), 303-328. doi:10.1002/jcop.20150

Perrow, C. (1984). *Normal accidents: Living with high-risk technologies*. Princeton, NJ: Princeton University Press.

Pieper, S. (2013). Charleston documentary shows how leadership and vision led to change. *Fire Fighter Nation*. Retrieved from http://www.firefighternation.com/article/management-and-leadership/charleston-documentary-shows-how-leadership-and-vision-led-change

Piotrowski, C. (2010). Earthquake in Haiti: The failure of crisis management. *Organizational Development Journal, 28*(1), 107-112. Retrieved from http://www.emeraldinsight.com/products/journals/journals.htm?id=lodj

Procee, H. (2006). Reflection in education: A Kantian epistemology. *Educational Theory, 56*(3), 237-253. doi:10.1111/j.1741-5446.2006.00225.x

Quinn, S. (2008). Crisis and emergency risk communication in a pandemic: A model for building capacity and resilience of minority communities. *Health Promotion Practice, 9*(4), 18S-25S. doi:10.1177/1524839908324022

Redding, J. (1997). Hardwiring the learning organization. *Training and Development, 51*(8), 61–67. Retrieved from http://www.traininganddevelopmentjournal.com/

Rizescu, M. (2011). Organizational culture influences on the organizations' functionality. *Revista Academiei Fortelor Terestre, 16*(1), 75-82. Retrieved from http://www.readperiodicals.com/201101/2300043371.html

Rochlin, G. I. (1991). Iran Air Flight 655 and the USS Vincennes: Complex, large scale military systems and the failure of control. In T. R. La Porte (Ed.), *Social responses to large technical systems: Control or anticipation.* Amsterdam, The Netherlands: Kluwer Academic Publishers.

Routley, J. G., Chiaramonte, M. D., Crawford, B. A., Piringer, P. A., Roche, K. M., & Sendelbach, T. E. (2008). Firefighter fatality investigative report. Retrieved from http://www.dps.state.ia.us

Sahaya, N. (2012). A learning organization as a mediator of leadership style and firms' financial performance. *International Journal of Business & Management, 7*(14), 96-113. Retrieved from http://www.ccsenet.org/journal/index.php/ijbm

Scanlan, M. (2011). Organizational learning in schools pursuing social justice: Fostering educational entrepreneurship and boundary spanning. *Scholar-Practitioner Quarterly, 5*(4), 328-346. Retrieved from epublications.marquette.edu/cgi/viewcontent.cgi?article=1177&context=edu_fac

Schein, E. H. (1992). *Organizational culture and leadership* (2nd ed.). San Francisco, CA: Jossey-Bass.

Schilling, J., & Kluge, A. (2009). Barriers to organizational learning: An integration of theory and research. *International Journal of Management Reviews, 11*(3), 337-360. doi:10.1111/j.1468-2370.2008.00242.x

Seeger, M. (2006). Best practices in crisis communication: An expert panel process. *Journal of Applied Communication Research, 34*(3), 232-244. doi:10.1080/00909880600769944

Sendelbach, T. (2012). FireRescue Magazine / Firefighter Nation. Retrieved from http://www.backstepfirefighter.com

Sendelbach, T. (2013). Telling the Charleston Fire Department's story of change. Retrieved from http://www.firefighternation. com/article/management-and-leadership/telling-charleston-fire-department-s-story-change

Senge, P. M. (1990). *The fifth discipline: The art and practice of learning organization*. New York, NY: Doubleday Dell.

Shen, Q. (2009). Case study in contemporary research: Conceptualization and critique. *Cross-Cultural Communication, 5*(4), 21-31. Retrieved from http://cscanada.net/index.php/ccc

Shrivastava, P., Mitroff, I. I., Miller, D., & Miglani, A. (1988). Understanding organizational crisis. *Journal of Management Studies, 25*, 285-303. Retrieved from http://onlinelibrary.wiley.com/jour nal/10.1111/%28ISSN%291467-6486

Shuhui Sophy, C., & Seeger, M. W. (2012). Lessons learned from organizational crisis: Business ethics and corporate communication. *International Journal of Business & Management, 8*(12), 74-86. doi:10.5539/ijbm.v7n12p74

Sikisch, G. (1995). *Emergency management planning handbook*. New York, NY: McGraw-Hill.

Simola, S. K. (2005). Organizational crisis management: Overview and opportunities. *Consulting Psychology Journal: Practice and Research, 57*(3), 180-192. doi:10.1037/1065-9293.57.3.180

Siomkos, G. J. (1992). Conceptual and methodological propositions for assessing responses to industrial crises. *Review of Business, 13*(4), 26–37. Retrieved from http://www.stjohns.edu/academics/ graduate/tobin/research/review

Smith, D. (1990). Beyond contingency planning: Towards a model of crisis management. *Organization and Environment, 4*(4),

263-275. doi:10.1177/108602669000400402

Smith, G., & Elmore, C. (2013). *Textbook Firefighting. The Post and Courier*, A1-A4. Retrieved from http://www.postandcourier.com/article/20130403/PC16/130409811/1005/crews-remain-on-the-scene-of-east-bay-street-fire-blaze-controlled

Snyder, P., Hall, M., Robertson, J., Jasinski, T., & Miller, J. (2006). Ethical rationality: A strategic approach to organizational crisis. *Journal of Business Ethics, 63*(4), 371-383. doi:10.1007/s10551-005-3328-9

Soliman, F. (2011). Could one transformational leader convert the organization from knowledge based into learning organization, then into innovation? *Journal of Modern Accounting & Auditing, 7*(12), 1352-1361. Retrieved from http://www.davidpublishing.com/davidpublishing/Upfile/2/29/2012/2012022903169616.pdf

Somers, S. (2009). Measuring resilience potential: An adaptive strategy for organizational crisis planning. *Journal of Contingencies & Crisis Management, 17*(1), 12-23. doi:10.1111/j.1468-5973.2009.00558.x

Song, J., Joo, B., & Chermack, T. J. (2009). The Dimensions of the Learning Organization Questionnaire (DLOQ): A validation study in a Korean context. *Human Resource Development Quarterly, 20*(1), 43-64. doi:10.1002/hrdq.20007

Stake, R. E. (1995). *The art of case study research*. London: Sage Publications.

Stake, R. E. (2003). *Case studies. Strategies of qualitative inquiry* (2nd ed.). London: Sage Publications.

Staw, B. M., Sandelands, L. E., & Dutton, J. E. (1981). Threat-rigidity effects in organizational behavior: A multi-level analysis.

Administration Science Quarterly, 26(4), 501-524. Retrieved from http://webuser.bus.umich.edu/janedut/Issue%20Selling/Staw%20et%20al%20threadt%20rigidity.pdf

Sutcliffe, K., & Vogus, T. (2003). Organizing for resilience. In K. Cameron (Ed.), *Positive organizational scholarship* (pp. 94-110). San Francisco, CA: Berrett-Koehler Publishers, Inc.

Taft, D. K. (2011). Never again: Today's FDNY is stronger and better prepared. *Eweek, 28*(14), 16-22. Retrieved from http://www.eweek.com/c/a/Government-IT/FDNY-Fortifies-Communications-IT-Systems-in-a-Post911-World-690496/

Tellis, W. (1997). Introduction to case study. *The Qualitative Report, 3*(2). Retrieved from http://www.nova.edu/ssss/QR/QR3-2/tellis1.html

Tierney, K., Lindell, M., & Perry, R. (2001). *Facing the unexpected.* Washington, DC: Joseph Henry Press.

Tieyang, Y., Sengul, M., & Lester, R. H. (2008). Misery loves company: The spread of negative impacts resulting from an organizational crisis. *Academy of Management Review, 33*(2), 452-472. doi:10.5465/AMR.2008.31193499.

Toloie-Eshlaghy, A., Chitsaz, S., Karimian, L., & Charkhchi, R. (2011). A classification of qualitative research methods. *Research Journal of International Studies, 20,* 106-123. Retrieved from http://gulib.georgetown.edu/newjour/r/msg02689.html

Toulabi, Z., Dehghani, M., & Al Taha, H. (2013). A survey of the relationship between organizational memory and organizational learning in public organizations of Kerman. *International Business Research, 6*(1), 90-96. doi:10.5539/ibr.v6n1p90

United States Fire Administration. (2013). Working for a safe

America. Retrieved from http://www.usfa.fema.gov/fireservice/
fatalities/statistics/casualties.shtm

Wallen, N. E., & Fraenkel, J. R. (2001). *Educational research: A guide to the process* (2nd ed.). Mahwah, NJ: Lawrence Erlbaum Associates.

Watkins, K. E., & Marsick, V. J. (1993). Organizational learning and the learning organization: A dichotomy between descriptive and perspective research. *Human Relations, 50,* 73-89. Retrieved from http://hum.sagepub.com/

Watkins, K., & Marsick, V. (1997). *Dimensions of the learning organization questionnaire.* Retrieved from http://www.partnersfor-learning.com/instructions.html

Watkins, K., & Marsick, V. (1997). *Dimensions of the Learning Organization Questionnaire.* Warwick, RI: Partners for the Learning Organization.

Watkins, K. E., & Marsick, V. (2003). Make learning count! Diagnosing the learning culture in organizations. *Advances in Developing Human Resources, 5*(2). Retrieved from http://adh.sagepub.com/

Webb, E. J., Campbell, D. T., Schwartz, R. D., & Sechrest, L. (1966). *Unobtrusive measures: Nonreactive measures in the social sciences.* Chicago, IL: Rand McNally.

Weick, K. E. (1988). Enacted sense making in crisis situations. *Journal of Management Studies, 25*(4), 305-317. Retrieved from http://onlinelibrary.wiley.com/journal/10.1111/%28ISSN%291467-6486

Weick, K. E. (1995). *Sensemaking in organizations.* Thousand Oaks, CA: Sage Publications.

Weick, K., & Sutcliffe, K. M. (2001). *Managing the unexpected:*

Assuring high performance in an age of complexity. San Francisco, CA: Jossey-Bass.

Wenger, D., Quarantelli, E. L., & Dynes, R. (1986). *Disaster analysis: Local emergency management offices and arrangements.* Newark, DE: Disaster Research Center. University of Delaware.

Wildavsky, A. (1988). *Searching for safety.* New Brunswick, CT: Transaction Books.

Wolensky, R., & Wolensky, K. (1991). American local government and the disaster management problem. *Local Government Studies, 17*(2), 15-32. doi:10.1080/03003939108433570

Yang, B., Watkins, K. E., & Marsick, V. J. (1998). Examining construct validity of the Dimensions of the Learning Organization Questionnaire. In R. Torraco (Ed.), *Proceedings of the 1998 Annual Academy of Human Resource Development Conference* (pp. 83-90). Chicago, IL: Academy of Human Resource Development.

Yang, B., Watkins, K. E., & Marsick, V. J. (2004). The construct of the learning organization: Dimensions, measurement, and validation. *Human Resource Development Quarterly, 15*(1), 31-55. doi:10.1002/hrdq.1086

Yeo, R. K. (2007). Change interventions to organizational learning: Bravo to leaders as unifying agents. *The Learning Organization, 14*(6), 524-552. doi:10.1108/09696470710825132

Yeung, A., Lai, K., & Yee, R. Y. (2007). Organizational learning, innovativeness, and organizational performance: A qualitative investigation. *International Journal of Production Research, 45*(11), 2459-2477. doi:10.1080/00207540601020460

Yin, R. K. (2003). *Case study research: Design and methods* (3rd ed.).

London: Sage Publications.

Yin, R. K. (2009). *Case study research: Design and method.* Thousand Oaks, CA: Sage Publications.

Young, S. (2007). *Comparing best practice cases in creating an environment conducive to development benefits, growth and investment.* Paper presented at the United Nations Conference on Trade and Development, Geneva, Switzerland.

Zhang, D., Zhang, Z., & Yang, B. (2004). Learning organization in mainland China: Empirical research on its application to Chinese state-owned enterprises. *International Journal of Training and Development, 8*(4), 258-273. doi:10.1111/j.1360-3736.2004.00213.x

APPENDIX A

City of Charleston

South Carolina

JOSEPH P. RILEY, JR.
MAYOR

KAREN E. BRACK
CHIEF

Fire Department

November 16, 2012

Office of Academic Research
Grand Canyon University
College of Doctoral Studies
3300 W. Camelback Road
Phoenix, AZ 85017
Phone: 602-639-7804

Dear IRB Members,

After reviewing the proposed study, *"Organizational Crisis in The City of Charleston Fire Department: An organizational learning and sense making approach"*, presented by *David Griffin*, I have granted authorization for *David Griffin* to conduct research at *The City of Charleston Fire Department*.

I understand the purpose of the study is to *provide research to fire service organizations regarding possible organizational crises following a line of duty death.* David Griffin will conduct the following research activities: *recruit, contact, and collect data.* It is understood that this project will end no later than *July 2013.*

I have indicated to David Griffin that my company will allow the following research activities: *participants will not complete the questionnaire during work hours. They will be completed in their own time at their home or designated private location of their choice.*

To ensure that the employees are protected, *David Griffin,* has agreed to provide to me a copy of any Grand Canyon University IRB-approved, consent document before s/he *recruits* participants at *The City of Charleston Fire Department. David Griffin* has agreed to provide a copy of the study results, in aggregate, to our college.

If the IRB has any concerns about the permission being granted by this letter, please contact me at the phone number listed below.

Sincerely,

Fire Chief

Karen E. Brack, Fire Chief
Printed Name
November 16, 2012
Signature Date

FC 12-01

APPENDIX B

Permission to use The Dimensions of the Learning Organization Questionnaire

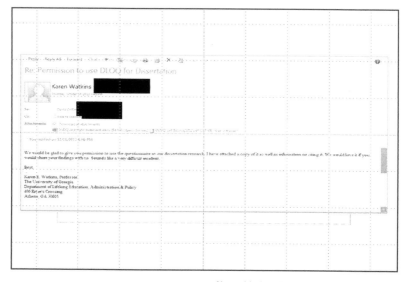

Note: this is a low resolution screen grab

APPENDIX C
Recruitment Letter

Crisis in The City of Charleston Fire Department:
An Organizational Learning Approach.

I am a graduate learner under the direction of Dr. Patricia Dolasinski in the Doctoral Program of Education at Grand Canyon University. I am conducting a qualitative case study to explore the organizational crisis that ensued after the June 18, 2007 multiple LODD's in The City of Charleston Fire Department. The study will be conducted with consideration to an organizational learning approach.

I am recruiting individuals to complete an online anonymous questionnaire from Dr. Watkins and Dr. Marsick entitled The Dimensions of The Learning Organization Questionnaire, which will take approximately one hour. Five of the participants will then be randomly selected for an interview with the researcher.

Your participation in this study is voluntary. If you have any questions concerning the research study, or are interested please call me at ▊▊▊▊▊ or email me at ▊▊▊▊▊. Thank you so much for your consideration to participate in the study.

David Griffin

APPENDIX D

Consent Form
Crisis in The City of Charleston Fire Department:
An Organizational Learning Approach

INTRODUCTION

The purposes of this form are to provide you (as a prospective research study participant) information that may affect your decision as to whether or not to participate in this research and to record the consent of those who agree to be involved in the study.

RESEARCH

David Griffin has invited your participation in a research study.

STUDY PURPOSE

The purpose of this qualitative case study is to indicate how an organization like the CFD learned from an organizational crisis at the individual, team, and organizational levels in The City of Charleston Fire Department in South Carolina following June 18, 2007. The study will be conducted through the perceptions of those involved through the lens of organizational learning.

DESCRIPTION OF RESEARCH STUDY

If you decide to participate, then as a study participant you will join a study involving research of the qualitative nature. Participants will be sent an email with a link to complete The Dimensions of the Learning Organization Questionnaire (DLOQ). Participants are allowed to skip questions if they feel it is appropriate. The study is anonymous and no personal information will be required of the participants. Upon completion of the questionnaire, the participants submit the questionnaire. Upon submission, the questionnaire is automatically emailed back to the researcher free of any personal information. If you say YES, then your participation will last for approximately 1 hour on your own computer in a private location of your choice. Five participants will then be randomly selected for an interview with the researcher. Approximately 27 subjects will be participating in this study from The City of Charleston Fire Department. This research will add to the body of knowledge of organizational crisis and organizational learning. Furthermore, this research will benefit fire service organizations not only after a line of duty death, but in an effort to prevent a tragic event such as June 18, 2007.

RISKS

There are no known risks from taking part in this study, but in any research, there is some possibility that you may be subject to risks that have not yet been identified.

BENEFITS

Although there may be no direct benefits to you, the possible benefit of your participation in the research is to offer other fire service organizations, as well as society, research regarding what takes place organizationally following a line of duty death.

NEW INFORMATION

If the researcher finds new information during the study that would reasonably change your decision about participating, then they will provide this information to you.

CONFIDENTIALITY

All information obtained in this study is strictly confidential. The results of this research study may be used in reports, presentations, and publications, but the researcher will not identify you. In order to maintain confidentiality of your records, David Griffin will keep the names of the participants confidential by utilizing subject codes. Since the questionnaire will be filled out on a third party website, which asks for no personal information, it will be impossible for anyone to ascertain the participant's answers. More importantly, the only individual that will have knowledge of the participant's identities is the researcher. All consent forms will be secured in a locked safe inside the researcher's safe room in his home. No other individuals will have access to the records of the participants. Upon completion of the study, the consent forms with the participant's names, as well as all other information not published in the study will be burned to ensure no chance of identification.

WITHDRAWAL PRIVILEGE

Participation in this study is completely voluntary. It is ok for you to say no. Even if you say yes now, you are free to say no later, and withdraw from the study at any time. Non-participation or withdrawal from the study will not affect your employment status. If you decide to withdraw, all of your information will be burned to ensure no identification is possible.

COSTS AND PAYMENTS

There is no payment for your participation in the study.

VOLUNTARY CONSENT

Any questions you have concerning the research study or your participation in the study, before or after your consent, will be answered by David Griffin. If you have questions about your rights as a subject/participant in this research, or if you feel you have been placed at risk, you can contact the Chair of the Institutional Review Board, through the College of Doctoral Studies at (602) 639-7804.

This form explains the nature, demands, benefits and any risk of the project. By signing this form you agree knowingly to assume any risks involved. Remember, your participation is voluntary. You may choose not to participate or to withdraw your consent and discontinue participation at any time without penalty or loss of benefit. In signing this consent form, you are not waiving any legal claims, rights, or remedies. A copy of this consent form will be given (offered) to you.

Your signature below indicates that you consent to participate in the above study.

_____

Subject's Signature / Printed Name / Date

_____

Other Signature / Printed Name / Date (if appropriate)

APPENDIX E

Confidentiality Agreement
Crisis in The City of Charleston Fire Department:
An Organizational Learning Approach.

As a researcher working on the above research study at Grand Canyon University, I understand that I must maintain the confidentiality of all information concerning research participants. This information includes, but is not limited to, all identifying information and research data of participants and all information accruing from any direct or indirect contact I may have with said participants. In order to maintain confidentiality, I hereby agree to refrain from discussing or disclosing any information regarding research participants, including information described without identifying information, to any individual who is not part of the above research study or in need of the information for the expressed purposes on the research program.

_____

Signature of Researcher / Printed Name / Date

_____

Signature of Witness / Printed Name / Date (if appropriate)

DLOQ PARTICIPANT MEAN RATINGS

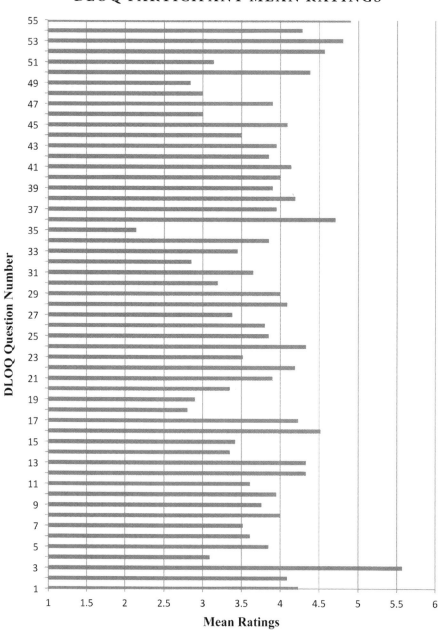

Made in the USA
Lexington, KY
15 December 2019